BIG ENGLISH 3 PLUS

Contents

Wake Up!

1 **What's missing in the pictures? Match and write.**

do   eat   play

1

a   She _____
in the morning.

2

b   She _____
in the afternoon.

3

c   She _____
after school.

2 **Read and circle.**

1 wake **up / off**

2 go **home / to home**

3 go to **park / the park**

4 go **school / to school**

5 **get / go** dressed

6 **watch / see** TV

3 **Listen and write. Then match.**

Hurry, Kate!

a

It's Monday, ¹____.
Kate has to wake up.
Her mum sees the clock and says
Wake up sleepy head.

Go, go, go! Hurry, Kate!
Hurry, Kate! You can't be late!

Kate eats breakfast, she gets dressed.
It's ²____.
It's time to go to school.
And she can't be late!

Chorus

Kate's got her backpack
And she's got her lunch.
What time is it now?
Oh, no, it's time to go!

Chorus

b

4 **Find out. Answer and draw. When does your friend wake up?**

_____

_____

5 **Read and circle.**

1	seven o'clock	**a** 7:00	**b** 6:00	
2	five twenty-five	**a** 2:25	**b** 5:25	
3	four forty-five	**a** 4:05	**b** 4:45	
4	two thirty	**a** 2:30	**b** 2:13	

6 Read. Write T for true and F for false.

I Love Mondays!

It's Monday and Luke wakes up. He says "Hooray! I love Mondays!" On Mondays, he's got Art at 11:10 before lunch. After lunch, at 2:15, he's got English. After school, he plays football or basketball. Luke eats breakfast and gets dressed. He puts on his shoes. He's ready for school but today there's no school. It's a holiday!

1 Today is Monday. _____   **2** Luke has got Art after school. _____

3 He's got English before lunch. _____   **4** He's ready for school. _____

5 He plays football after school. _____   **6** He goes to school today. _____

7 Write about you. What do you do before school and after school?

1 Before school, _____.

2 After school, _____.

THINK BIG

What does Luke do next? Draw and write.

Luke _____

_____

_____.

10

8 **Listen and stick. Number the pictures and answer.**

a

When does she go to bed?

_____

b

When does she go to school?

_____

c

When does she eat breakfast?

_____

d

When does she wake up?

_____

9 **Correct the sentences for you.**

1 I do my homework in the morning.

_____

2 I eat breakfast at 9:30.

_____

3 I go home at 4:45.

_____

4 I play basketball after school.

_____

5 I watch TV in the morning, afternoon and evening.

_____

10 **Read. Then write before or after.**

wakes up   eats breakfast   gets dressed   goes to school

does homework   watches TV   goes to bed

1 Susan eats breakfast _____ she wakes up.

2 She wakes up _____ she gets dressed.

3 She gets dressed _____ she goes to school.

4 She does her homework _____ she goes to school.

5 She does her homework _____ she watches TV.

6 She goes to bed _____ she does her homework.

11 **Write the answers.**

1 What does your brother or sister do before school?

_____

2 What does your brother or sister do after school?

_____

3 What does your mum or dad do before school?

_____

4 What does your mum or dad do after school?

_____

12 **Look and complete the chart.**

bath   face   hair   hands   shower   teeth

have/take a	wash your	brush your	brush/comb your

13 **Listen and write. Then match the pictures a–c to paragraphs 1–3.**

Bacteria   decay   Dirty   shower   sneeze   wash

1   It's important that we are clean every day. We can have a bath or a ¹ _____. We must always use warm water to ² _____ away dirt, sweat, dead skin and bacteria. Bacteria are very, very small and live on our skin. We can't see them but they can make us ill.

a

2   We must brush our teeth every day for about two minutes. Brush them in the morning and before you go to bed. ³ _____ can cause tooth ⁴ _____ and gum disease, so brushing our teeth keeps them strong and healthy.

b

3   We have to keep our hands clean, too. ⁵ _____ hands have germs that make us ill. We need to wash our hands with soap before we eat, after we go to the toilet, or when we cough or ⁶ _____.

c

14 **Find and write the words.**

ieraacbt

iseedas

trydi

1 _____

2 _____

3 _____

swtea

sgrem

4 _____

5 _____

15 **Read and match.**

1 We brush our   water and soap   to wash away bacteria.

2 We use   hands   after we cough or sneeze.

3 We wash our   teeth   to stop gum disease.

16 **Put the words in order.**

1 | germs | leaves | Coughing | on our hands. |

_____

2 | full | germs. | Sneezes | of | are |

_____

3 | hands. | clean | our | soap | water | Warm | and |

_____

4 | teeth | your | decay. | Brushing | tooth | stops |

_____

THINK BIG   **Where can you find germs? Put a ✓ or a ✗.**

☐ In the bathroom   ☐ In the garden   ☐ In the park

17 **Look at the chart. Circle T for true and F for false.**

	Linda	Jose	Melissa
Play basketball	5	3	5
Have a shower	3	1	4
Eat healthy food	4	2	2
Take the bus to school	1	5	3
Go to bed before 10 p.m.	2	4	5

I Always   2 Usually   3 Often   4 Sometimes   5 Never

1 Linda usually goes to bed before 10 p.m.   **T**   **F**

2 Melissa often takes the bus to school.   **T**   **F**

3 Melissa always has a shower.   **T**   **F**

4 Linda never eats healthy food.   **T**   **F**

5 Jose often plays basketball.   **T**   **F**

6 Jose and Melissa usually eat healthy food.   **T**   **F**

18 **Look at 17. Make sentences with always, usually, often, sometimes or never.**

1 Linda and Melissa/play basketball

_____

2 Jose/have a shower

_____

3 Melissa/eat healthy food

_____

4 Jose and Melissa/eat healthy food

_____

5 Linda/take the bus to school

_____

6 Jose/go to bed before 10 p.m.

_____

19 Make questions.

1 you/sometimes/walk to school

_____? Yes, I do.

2 she/always/brush her teeth

_____? No, she doesn't.

3 they/usually/play in the park

_____? Yes, they do.

4 your dad/often/eat cereal for breakfast

_____? Yes, he does.

20 Make negative sentences.

1 I always play computer games.

_____

2 We often eat pasta for lunch.

_____

3 Sometimes I walk the dog.

_____

4 She often cleans her room.

_____

5 He usually goes to bed early.

_____

21 Read and complete.

away	of	on	to	with

1 We have to get rid _____ germs.
2 Bacteria live _____ our skin and in our mouth.
3 You have to wash _____ soap and water.
4 We need _____ stay clean and healthy.
5 We can wash the dirt _____ in the shower.

22 **Look at the times. Complete.**

New York — Manuel

Texas — Maria

Montana — John

California — Kara

1 It's one fifteen in New York. What time is it in Texas? _____

2 It's eleven fifteen in Montana. What time is it in California? _____

3 It's ten fifteen. Where am I? _____

4 It's twelve fifteen. Where am I? _____

15

23 **Listen and circle.**

1   Time isn't the same around the world. We live on a **¹ globe / circle** with different time **² days / zones**. For example, when it's day in Hong Kong, it's night in New York. When there's sun in New Zealand, it's dark in the U.K. Often these places are in a different **³ day / week**, too.

2   This is because the **⁴ Earth / Moon** makes half a full turn every 12 hours. This means New York sees its new day 12 hours after Hong Kong. There are often different **⁵ time / night** zones in the same country, too, such as in Russia or in the U.S.A. The U.S.A. has got four **⁶ different / big** time zones.

3   For example, when it's 10:30 a.m. for Kara in California, she's in class. She's had breakfast, so she isn't hungry yet. But John in Montana is getting hungry because it's 11:30 a.m. He wants his **⁷ breakfast / lunch** soon! It's already lunch time for Maria in Texas, where it's 12:30 p.m. And lunch is finished for Manuel, because the time in New York is 1:30 p.m.

24 **Look at 23. Circle T for true and F for false.**

1 We have night and day because the Earth turns.   T   F

2 All countries have the same time zones.   T   F

3 The U.S.A. is in the same time zone as Hong Kong.   T   F

4 Countries can be in different days because of time zones.   T   F

5 When it's 10:30 in California, it's 12:30 in New York.   T   F

6 When Manuel has finished lunch, John is getting hungry.   T   F

25 **Write the times using words.**

1 (10:10/London) _____.

2 (12:30/Paris) _____.

3 (18:00/Cairo) _____.

4 (17:25/Beijing) _____.

5 (21:45/Tokyo) _____.

26 **Read and answer.**

It's 1:00 a.m. in London. What time is it in...

1 Los Angeles (-8 hours) _____   5 Moscow (+3 hours) _____

2 Mexico City (-6 hours) _____   6 Singapore (+7 hours) _____

3 Boston (-5 hours) _____   7 Sydney (+11 hours) _____

4 Istanbul (+2 hours) _____   8 Buenos Aires (-4 hours) _____

TH■NK BiG

Do you know anyone who lives in another time zone? Where are they? What's the time difference?

Name: _____   Lives: _____

Time difference: + / - _____ hours

27 **How many subjects and how many verbs can you find?**

Julie wakes up at 6:45. Then she eats breakfast. She washes her face. She brushes her teeth. She gets dressed. She goes to school at 8:30.

28 **Underline the subject.**

1 Jeff wakes up at 6:45 in the morning.
2 We go to school at 7:30 in the morning.
3 I feed my cat before school.
4 Carol does the dishes in the evening.
5 He plays basketball in the afternoon.

29 **Underline the verb.**

1 I make my bed before school.
2 He rides his bike to school.
3 They play video games after school.
4 My sister reads books every day.
5 My sister comes home at 3:45.

30 **Write about three family members. What do they do?**

Family Members			
My aunt	My brother	My cousin	My father
My mother	My sister	My uncle	

1 _____ in the morning.

2 _____ in the afternoon.

3 _____ in the evening.

31 **Read and circle a_e, i_e and o_e.**

face

bone

sheep

time

bike

soup

cake

note

32 **Underline the words with a_e, i_e and o_e. Then read aloud.**

1 The girl is eating a cake and the dog is eating a bone.

2 I love my bike and my board game.

33 **Connect the letters. Then write.**

1 f

2 l

3 b

one   **a** _ _ _ _

ace   **b** _ _ _ _

ike   **c** _ _ _ _

20

34 **Listen and write.**

What time is it?

It's time to play a ¹_____.

What time is it?

It's time to eat ²_____.

What time is it?

It's time to ride a ³_____.

What time is it?

It's time to go ⁴_____.

35 **Match and write sentences for you. Use before or after.**

1 wash my   **a** a shower   _____

2 wash   **b** my teeth   _____

3 take   **c** face   _____

4 brush   **d** hair   _____

5 comb my   **e** my hands   _____

36 **Put the words in order. Find out and then answer.**

1 | does | When | wake | your dad | up? | usually |

_____

_____

2 | When | her hands? | does | wash | your mum |

_____

_____

3 | bed | your parents | Do | go to | always | at 9 p.m.? |

_____

_____

4 | it | What | is | time | now? |

_____

_____

5 | you | watch TV | sometimes | Do | on Saturday? |

_____

_____

Lots of Jobs!

1 Follow the paths and write the jobs.

1 hospital

2 laboratory

3 Moe's farm

4 restaurant

a _____

b _____

c _____

d _____

2 Listen and number in order from 1–5. Then circle all the jobs.

Working Together

Working together, working hard.
Nurse, farmer, teacher and chef.

Where does he work?
What does he do?
He's a firefighter
And he's very brave, too.

There are many people
In our community.
So many jobs to do,
So many places to be.

Where does she work?
What does she do?
She's a nurse
And she always helps you.

Working together, working hard.
Nurse, farmer, teacher and chef.

3 Read and circle T for true and F for false.

1 A firefighter works on a farm.   T   F

2 A waiter works at a restaurant.   T   F

3 A police officer works at a shop.   T   F

4 A student studies at a university.   T   F

5 A cashier works at a laboratory.   T   F

4 Choose a job and draw. Then answer.

What does he/she do?

_____

_____

Where does he/she work?

_____

_____

5 **Read. Then circle.**

Is She a Doctor?

Luke and his dad are at the hospital. They are looking for Luke's mum. Luke's mum works at the hospital. But she isn't a doctor. She's a cashier. She works in the hospital gift shop. Today's her birthday!

1 Luke is looking for **a nurse / his mum**.

2 Luke's mum works at the **post office / hospital**.

3 Luke's mum is a **doctor / cashier**.

4 She works in the **gift shop / supermarket**.

6 **Answer the questions about a family member.**

1 What does he or she do? _____

2 Where does he or she work? _____

THINK BIG

How does Luke's mum celebrate her birthday? What does she do? Draw and write.

_____

_____

_____

29

7 🎧 **Listen and stick. Then number.**

a

☐

b

☐

c

$x + 3y =$

☐

8 **Look and complete.**

1 **A:** What ¹_____ your brothers ²_____?

   B: They ³_____ firefighters.

   A: Where ⁴_____ they work?

   B: They ⁵_____ at the ⁶_____.

2 **A:** What ¹_____ your dad ²_____?

   B: He ³_____ a waiter.

   A: Where ⁴_____ he ⁵_____?

   B: He ⁶_____ at a Spanish ⁷_____.

Language in Action

9 **Listen and ✓.**

1 What does Peggy's dad do?

He's ☐ a cashier. ☐ a teacher. ☐ a farmer.

2 Where does Peggy's mum work?

She works ☐ at a restaurant. ☐ at a police station. ☐ at a fire station.

3 Where does Peggy's brother work?

He works ☐ at a laboratory. ☐ at a university. ☐ at a school.

4 What does her sister do?

She's ☐ a chef. ☐ a student. ☐ a police officer.

10 **Read and write Where or What.**

1 **A:** _____ does your brother work?
B: He works at a post office.

2 **A:** _____ does your sister do?
B: She's a nurse.

3 **A:** _____ do you do?
B: I'm a scientist.

4 **A:** _____ do your parents work?
B: They work on a farm.

11 **Put the words in order.**

1 does uncle What do? your

_____

2 waiter. He's a

_____

3 at He a works restaurant.

_____

12 **Read and match.**

1 Susie is a fashion designer.

2 Jake is an artist.

3 Mark is a photographer.

a   b   c

33

13 **Listen, read and complete.**

camera creative fashion galleries job sketches work

1   We spend a lot of time at ¹ _____, so it's important to choose a ² _____ we enjoy. Here are some creative jobs.

2   Professional artists study first at art school. They learn to be ³ _____ with different materials. Artists draw with pencils, or paint with oil paints, acrylics or watercolours. They sometimes use metal or wood to make other works of art. Some artists use unusual materials like chewing gum, buttons or even plastic supermarket bags! Artists show their work in ⁴ _____.

3   Photographers take pictures of people, places and things all over the world. Good photographers always have a ⁵ _____ with them. They sell their photos to websites, newspapers, magazines and television news programmes. Their photos are also used in books.

4   Fashion designers design the clothes we wear. They have good ideas and draw ⁶ _____ of them. Then they cut patterns to make clothes, such as dresses, trousers or coats. We see their work in ⁷ _____ shows or at photo shoots for magazines. We can buy their clothes in shops or online.

14 **Look at 13. Circle T for true and F for false.**

1 Artists sometimes use chewing gum.   T   F

2 Galleries show art to the public.   T   F

3 Photographers design websites.   T   F

4 A good photographer always carries a camera. T   F

5 Fashion designers design cars.   T   F

15 **Look at 13. Match to make phrases from the text.**

1	chewing	a animals
2	plastic	b gum
3	art	c gallery
4	water	d shoot
5	wild	e show
6	fashion	f bag
7	photo	g colour

16 **Complete the crossword. Use the clues and the words from the box.**

designer   gallery   landscapes   photographer   sketch   upload

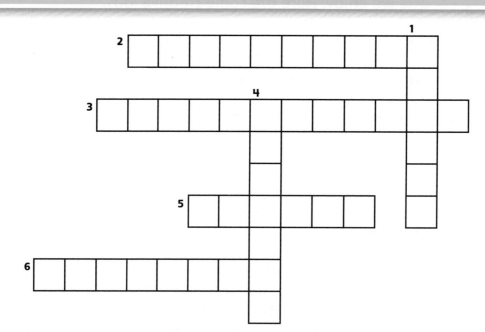

Down ↓

1 When Susie's got an idea she draws a ❓.

4 Jake shows his paintings in an art ❓.

Across →

2 Jake likes painting the mountains. He paints ❓.

3 A ❓ takes photos of people and places.

5 I ❓ my photos to the computer.

6 Susie loves drawing clothes. She's a fashion ❓.

THINK BIG

When fashion designers see people wearing their clothes, they feel happy. When do you feel happy?

When I _____, I feel happy.

17 **Read and write.**

> am   is   live   look   study   wants   work   works

I ¹ _____ a scientist and I ² _____
at a laboratory at the university. I usually work from
9 a.m. to 5 or 6 p.m. but sometimes I stay late and
I ³ _____. My friend ⁴ _____ a
nurse and ⁵ _____ at the local hospital.
Sometimes he also stays late. I want to
⁶ _____ on a farm one day. My friend
likes farms, too. He ⁷ _____ to
⁸ _____ after animals instead of people!

18 **Choose the correct word and ✓.**

1 I   ☐ study   at night.
        ☐ studies

2 We ☐ live   on a farm.
        ☐ lives

3 She ☐ work   at a hospital.
        ☐ works

4 He ☐ travel   all over the world.
        ☐ travels

5 They ☐ stay   at Park Hotel.
        ☐ stays

6 They ☐ love   animals.
        ☐ loves

Grammar

19 **Look and write. What do they do?**

1 He's a _____

2 _____

3 _____

4 _____

5 _____

6 _____

20 **Write questions and answers.**

1 **A:** _____ (he/work/hospital)

B: _____. _____ fire station.

2 **A:** _____ (she/work/police station)

B: _____. _____ school.

3 **A:** _____ (you/eat/restaurant)

B: _____. _____ home.

4 **A:** _____ (Dad/play football/Saturday)

B: _____. _____ Friday.

5 **A:** _____ (they/live/Madrid)

B: _____. _____ Barcelona.

21 **Read. Find the three countries.**

Lalana lives in Thailand. She helps schools. Lalana and her friends ask people for books. They give the books to schools.

Marcus lives in Australia. Marcus and his friends clean up the streets. They pick up rubbish before school.

Carla lives in Spain. Carla and her big sister help tourists. Tourists visit Spain. They get lost. Carla and her big sister find the places they're looking for.

36

22 **Listen, read and complete. Use the words from the box.**

clean	collect	community	donate	helping	lost	rubbish	world

1   A lot of people say they want to make the ¹ _____ a better place. Many don't do anything, but many do lots of useful and helpful things. Start with where you live. When you do good things to help your ² _____, you help the world, too.

2   In Chiang Mai, Thailand, many schools don't have money to buy books. Lalana and her friends help by asking people to ³ _____ books. They ⁴ _____ the books and take them to schools in their city. Now the schools have books.

3   In Melbourne, Australia, Marcus sees ⁵ _____ on the roads when he walks to school. So he and his friends pick up the rubbish. They have contests to see who can collect the most. They keep the streets ⁶ _____ and it's fun.

4   In Barcelona, Spain, Carla helps tourists when they get ⁷ _____. She loves her city and she likes ⁸ _____ people. She and her sister help tourists at weekends.

23 **Look at 22. Read and match. Then choose and complete.**

| Carla and her sister | Lalana and her friends | Marcus and his friends |

1 _____ collect books

a the streets clean.

2 _____ keep

b who can pick up the most rubbish.

3 _____ have contests to see

c tourists at weekends.

4 _____ help

d and take them to schools.

24 **Read and write.**

| about   for   in   to   with |

1 To make the world a better place, start _____ where you live.
2 Let's do something _____ it!
3 They have better books, thanks _____ Lalana and her friends.
4 We help tourists look _____ places to visit.
5 He picks up rubbish _____ the streets.

Can you help your community? What can you do? Write and draw.

I can help _____

_____

_____

_____ .

25 **Circle the subjects and underline the verbs.**

Steve and Mohammed are friends. They work at a laboratory. They play basketball and watch TV on a Saturday.

26 **Rachel and Kate are sisters. Read and complete.**

Rachel
I am a police officer.
I dance.
I sing.
I live on a farm.

Kate
I am a teacher.
I dance.
I play the piano.
I live in a city.

1 _____ and _____ are sisters.

2 _____ and _____ dance.

3 _____ dances and sings.

4 _____ dances and plays the piano.

5 _____ lives in a city.

6 _____ lives on a farm.

27 **Write about you.**

I _____ and _____ in the evening.

My friend and I _____ after school.

28 Read and circle sm, st, sk and sp.

> smile
>
> game
>
> spoon
>
> storm
>
> space
>
> smart
>
> ski star
>
> skate
>
> note

29 Underline the words with sm, st, sk and sp. Then read aloud.

1 There are small stars in space.

2 We skate and ski in winter.

30 Connect the letters. Then write.

1	sm	oon	**a**	_ _ _ _ _
2	sp	ar	**b**	_ _ _ _
3	st	i	**c**	_ _ _
4	sk	ile	**d**	_ _ _ _ _

41
31 Listen and write.

> ¹ _____ and look.
> Look at the ² _____,
> The stars in ³ _____,
> And ⁴ _____!

32 **Look and complete. Then answer.**

1 What _____ your sister do?

　　　☐ **a** She's a teacher.
　　　☐ **b** She's a police officer.

2 What _____ your mum _____?

　　　☐ **a** She's a waiter.
　　　☐ **b** She's a scientist.

3 What _____ your brothers do?

　　　☐ **a** They're firefighters.
　　　☐ **b** They're students.

4 What _____ your cousins _____?

　　　☐ **a** They're nurses.
　　　☐ **b** They're farmers.

33 **Read and match.**

1 I like dancing. When I

2 When they take a photo, they

3 When she's got an idea,

4 When he sees a beautiful landscape,

5 I get ideas when

a she draws a sketch.

b dance, I feel happy.

c he paints it.

d I go to an art gallery.

e upload it to a computer.

unit 3

Working Hard!

1 **Follow and write. Use the words from the box.**

bed   dishes   dog   fish
piano   room   rubbish   test

1   clean — my
2   do — the
3   feed — the
4   make — my
5   practise — the
6   study — for — a
7   take — out — the
8   walk — the

_____
_____
_____
_____
_____
_____
_____
_____

46

2 **Listen. What things do they do? Match. Then write.**

1   Tara _____
    _____.

2   Dave _____
    _____.

3   Christy _____
    _____.

4   Matt _____
    _____.

a

b

c

d

3 **Listen and circle.**

Different Twins

My name's Matt
And my name's Mike.
We want to talk to you.
I do my chores
And I do, too.
But we are not alike.

Mike and Matt, Matt and Mike.
These two twins are not alike.

I'm Matt,
I always **take out the rubbish / clean my room.**
I do my chores each day.
I sometimes **do the dishes / study for a test**
And then we go and play.

Chorus

I'm Mike,
I always **clean my room / make my bed.**
I do my chores each day.
I sometimes **feed the fish / walk the dog**
And then we go and play.

Chorus

4 **What chores do you do? Write four sentences.**

_____

_____

_____

_____

5 Read. Then number in order.

I Have a Lot to Do

Amy is thinking. She's making a list. She has to do lots of things before school. She has to eat breakfast. She has to brush her teeth. Then she has to feed her fish, clean her room and study for her Maths test. Amy goes to school at 7:50. Her alarm clock says 7:05. Mum says "It's 7:45." Amy's clock isn't working! She has to get a new alarm clock.

_____ She has to study for her Maths test.

_____ She has to feed the fish.

_____ She has to brush her teeth.

_____ Amy has to eat breakfast.

_____ She has to get a new alarm clock.

_____ She has to clean her room.

6 Write. What do you have to do before school?

I have to _____ before school.

Think and write for you.

THINK BIG

1 I have to _____ before I go to bed.

2 I have to _____ before I go to bed.

3 I have to _____ before I go to bed.

4 I have to _____ before I go to bed.

52

7 **Listen and stick.**

Monday	Tuesday	Wednesday	Thursday	Friday

8 **Read and circle the correct words.**

1 **A:** What **do / does** Nancy have to do after school?

B: She **have to / has to** practise the piano.

2 **A:** What **do / does** we have to do this evening?

B: We **have to / has to** study for our test tomorrow.

3 **A:** What **do / does** you have to do every morning?

B: I **have to / has to** make my bed.

9 **What do they have to do? Look and write.**

Kate and Ted   Jane   Jim and Mike

1 Kate: _____

2 Ted: _____

3 Jane: _____

4 Jim and Mike: _____

10 **Look and match.**

1 always

	Sun	Mon	Tue	Wed	Thurs	Fri	Sat
a							

2 usually

	Sun	Mon	Tue	Wed	Thurs	Fri	Sat
b							

3 sometimes

	Sun	Mon	Tue	Wed	Thurs	Fri	Sat
c							

4 never

	Sun	Mon	Tue	Wed	Thurs	Fri	Sat
d							

11 **Complete with always, usually, sometimes or never.**

1 I _____ feed the fish.

2 I _____ study for tests.

3 I _____ take out the rubbish.

4 I _____ do the dishes.

	M	T	W	T	F
feed the fish	✔		✔		✔
study for a test				✔	✔
take out the rubbish					
do the dishes	✔	✔	✔	✔	✔

12 **Complete for you. Use the verbs from the box.**

clean   do   make   practise   study   take

1 I usually _____.

2 I sometimes _____.

3 I never _____.

4 I always _____.

13 **Read and match.**

1 walk the   **a** plants

2 tidy the   **b** breakfast

3 take out the   **c** dog

4 water the   **d** room

5 wash   **e** rubbish

6 make   **f** the car

55

14 **Listen, read and write. Then check your answers in 13.**

buy   cash   earn   housework   pocket   safe   save

1   As children, we don't have money. Our parents usually [1] _____ the things we need. They sometimes give us some [2] _____ money, too. But soon, we want to buy things which cost more money and we need to find extra cash.

2   There's always lots to do around the house. Maybe you can ask your parents to give you some money for helping with the [3] _____? Or maybe you can earn [4] _____ by tidying your room, putting out the rubbish, making breakfast or doing the dishes.

3   You can also [5] _____ money by helping friends and neighbours. For example, you can help in the garden, or water the plants in the house. You can walk the dog or wash the car, too. Of course, you must make sure you're [6] _____. Don't work for strangers. Always tell your parents where you are, and ask to know that it's ok.

4   Then buy some nice things, but try to [7] _____ a little bit of the money you make every time. This way you always have extra cash.

15 **Look at 14. Circle T for true and F for false.**

1 Parents usually buy children the things they need.　　T　　F

2 There's never lots to do around the house.　　T　　F

3 Washing the dog is a good way to earn cash.　　T　　F

4 We should never work for strangers.　　T　　F

5 Saving some money is a bad idea.　　T　　F

16 **Put the words in order.**

1 | I | dog. | when | money | the | earn | walk | I |

_____

2 | when | cents | earns | dishes. | Nadia | fifty | she | the | does |

_____

3 | twice | cooked | week. | Alex | this | dinner |

_____

4 | morning | made | week. | this | every | bed | his | Erol |

_____

5 | earned | her | €4.50. | tidied | and | room | Rosa |

_____

I earn two euros each time I clean my room. I clean it twice a week. How much pocket money do I earn?

THINK BIG **Read and ✓.**

€2 x 1 = €2 ☐　€2 x 2 = €4 ☐　€1 x 3 = €3 ☐

Is it better to spend or save pocket money? Why?
How much of your pocket money should you save?

17 **Look at the chart. Circle T for true and F for false.**

	watch films	have parties	spend time at home	tidy up	walk the dog
Mike	***	***	**	*	***
Angela	****	***	***	*	****

**** love   *** like   ** not / like   * hate

1   Mike likes tidying up.   T   F

2   Mike loves walking the dog.   T   F

3   Angela likes spending time at home.   T   F

4   Mike loves having parties.   T   F

5   Angela loves watching films.   T   F

6   Angela hates tidying up.   T   F

18 **Look at 17. Write sentences.**

1   Angela/walk the dog

_____

2   Mike/watch films

_____

3   Mike/spend time at home

_____

4   Angela/tidy up

_____

5   Mike and Angela/have parties

_____

Grammar

19 **Write questions with like, love and hate.**

1 he/like/walk the dog?

_____

2 you/love/play football?

_____

3 she/hate/do the dishes?

_____

4 they/hate/tidy/their rooms?

_____

5 your cat/like/play/with a ball?

_____

20 **Write the -ing form.**

1 swim _____ **2** spend _____

3 sit _____ **4** give _____

5 feed _____ **6** let _____

7 take _____ **8** study _____

21 **Answer the questions about you. Use like, love and hate.**

1 Do you like watching action films?

Yes, I do. I love watching action films.

No, I don't like/hate watching action films. I love watching comedies.

2 Do you like doing homework?

_____

_____

3 Do you like washing the dishes?

_____

_____

4 Do you like playing football?

_____

_____

22 Read and match.

a

1 Leah lives in Alaska. She has to shovel snow before school.

b

2 Ivan lives on a farm. He has to feed the goats before school.

3 Chen Wei's mom has a noodle restaurant. He has to help his mother make noodles.

c

58
23 Listen, read and write.

> care   chores   clear   helps   keep   makes   task   tiring

1 Around the world, many children help their parents with ¹ _____. Some also do chores as part of life in a family business. Difficult tasks always become easy when you have help.

2 There's usually a lot of snow on the roads and the pavements in Alaska. Everyone has to shovel snow to ² _____ their entrances ³ _____. Leah shovels snow before she goes to school every day. She likes her ⁴ _____.

3 Ivan lives in France on a farm. He gets milk from the goats on his farm to make goat's cheese, and then he sells it. He ⁵ _____ his father to take ⁶ _____ of the goats. Every morning, he has to get up early to feed them. He goes to school after his work on the farm.

4 Chen Wei's mother ⁷ _____ the best noodles in Singapore. Everyone knows her and wants her noodles. People come from all over the country to try them. It's ⁸ _____ work in the kitchen, so after he does his homework, Chen Wei helps his mother. He also loves eating them!

24 **Look at 23. Read and circle.**

1 There is a lot of **noodles / snow** in Alaska.

2 People use **shovels / spoons** to clear it.

3 Ivan gets up **late / early** every day to work on the **road / farm**.

4 Chen Wei's mother makes the best noodles in **Singapore / China**. Chen Wei loves **selling / eating** them!

25 **Put the words in order.**

1 | lot | snow. | There | a | is | of |

_____

2 | clear | the | shovels | She | entrance. | snow | to |

_____

3 | the | They | make | cheese | farm. | on | goat |

_____

4 | get | every | has | to | early | morning. | up | He |

_____

5 | noodles | Making | work. | is | tiring |

_____

6 | his | Chen Wei | homework | mother. | he | before | helps | her | does |

_____

THINK BIG

Put a ✓ to the chores.

go to a party ☐   clean the kitchen ☐

play in the garden ☐   feed the fish ☐

walk the dog ☐   watch television ☐

make your bed ☐   listen to music ☐

26 **Read. Then ✗ the words we don't write in capitals.**

> Use **capital letters** for most words in titles.
> **I H**ave a **L**ot to **D**o!
>
> But always use capital letters for the first word in a title.
> **A** Day at the Park with Grandma

and, but, or, a, an, the   ☐

grandpa, mum, brother   ☐

at, for, in, on, to, with   ☐

big, good   ☐

help, walk, eat   ☐

Taking Care of a Big Dog

Good Things to Eat

My Brother and I

27 **Circle the title with the correct capitals.**

1 A big blue balloon
a Big Blue Balloon
A Big Blue Balloon

2 The Chef and the Waiter
the Chef and the Waiter
The Chef And The Waiter

3 Harry Needs a Helping Hand
Harry needs a Helping Hand
Harry Needs A Helping Hand

4 Dinner At Grandpa's House
Dinner at Grandpa's House
Dinner at grandpa's house

28 **Write the correct title. Use capital letters.**

1 _____

uncle Joe's dream
penguin trouble at the zoo
a surprise for grandma

2 _____

3 _____

29 **Read and circle ay and oy.**

> bike
>
> say
>
> day
>
> May
>
> boy
>
> toy
>
> stop
>
> joy

30 **Underline the words with ay and oy. Then read aloud.**

1 On Sundays we play all day with our toys.

2 I'm reading the story of a boy called Roy.

31 **Connect the letters. Then write.**

1 d   oy   **a** _ _ _

2 t   ay   **b** _ _ _

63

32 **Listen and write.**

What do we ¹ _____?

It's May, it's ² _____,

It's a nice ³ _____.

Come on, girls!

Come on, ⁴ _____!

Bring your ⁵ _____.

33 **Look, read and ✓.**

I clean my room three times a week. I get fifty cents each time. How much pocket money do I earn?

I take out the rubbish four times a week. I get one euro each time. How much pocket money do I earn?

50c x 2 = €1 ☐

€3 x 1= €3 ☐

50c x 3 = €1.50 ☐

€1 x 3= €3 ☐

€1 x 4= €4 ☐

50c x 3 = €1.50 ☐

34 **Look. Write T for true and F for false.**

Alicia's Chores	Monday	Tuesday	Wednesday	Thursday	Friday
make the bed	✓	✓	✓	✓	✓
do the dishes	✓		✓		
feed the fish	✓	✓	✓	✓	
take out the rubbish					

1 Alicia always makes the bed. _____

2 Alicia never does the dishes. _____

3 Alicia usually feeds the fish. _____

4 Alicia sometimes takes out the rubbish. _____

35 **Look and write about Josh and Adam. Use has to and have to.**

1 Josh and Adam _____

_____ dog.

2 _____

_____ piano.

	Josh	Adam
walk the dog	✓	✓
practise the piano	✓	
study for a test	✓	✓
clean his room		✓

3 _____ test.

4 _____ room.

Sue's Busy Day

1 **Choose one path. Draw the path. Learn about Sue's busy day.**

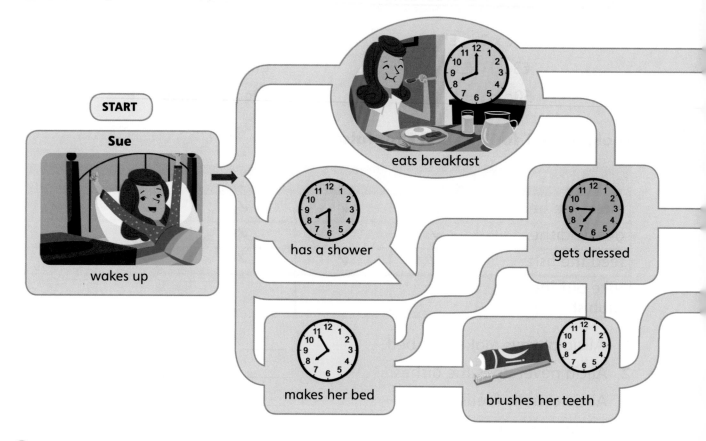

2 **Look at your path in 1. Guess and write.**

1 What time does Sue wake up? She wakes up at _____.

2 What does Sue do? She's a _____.

3 **Look at your path in 1. Write five sentences about Sue's day.**

1 _____

2 _____

3 _____

4 _____

5 _____

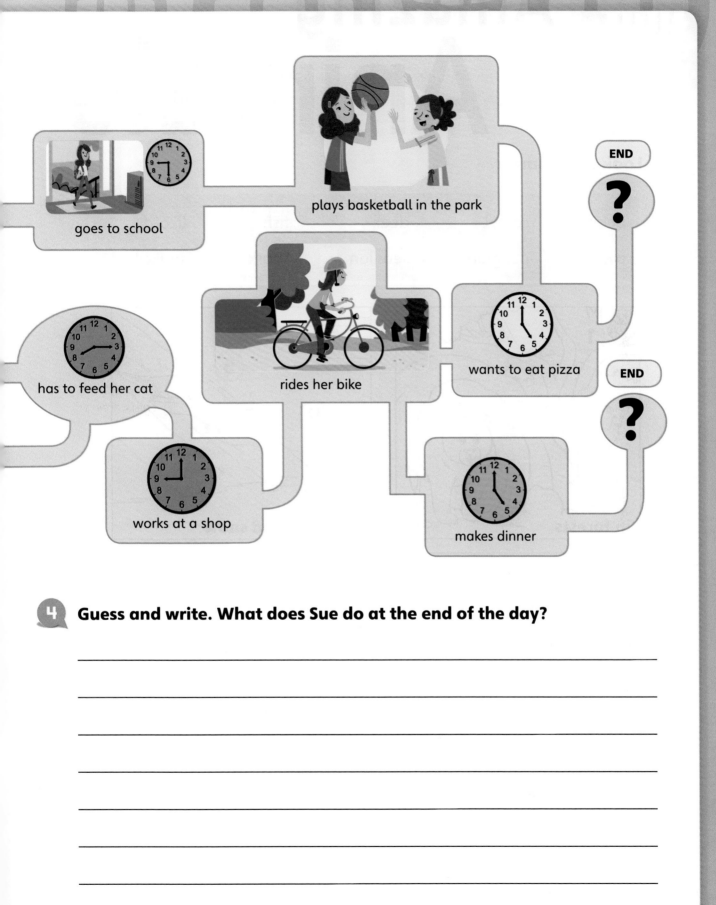

goes to school

plays basketball in the park

END
?

has to feed her cat

rides her bike

wants to eat pizza

END
?

works at a shop

makes dinner

4 **Guess and write. What does Sue do at the end of the day?**

_____

_____

_____

_____

_____

_____

unit 4 Amazing Animals

1 **Look and number.**

bear ☐   camel ☐   deer ☐   fish ☐   lizard ☐

owl ☐   penguin ☐   sea lion ☐   shark ☐   snake ☐

in forests

in the ice and snow

in deserts

in oceans

2 **Write.**

My favourite animals are _____.

They _____.

3 Listen and write. Then number. Underline the places.

a

□

b

□

c

□

d

□

e

□

Animals Are Amazing!

Animals are amazing!
We see them far and near.
Some live in forests
Like ¹ _____, ² _____
and ³ _____.

Some live in deserts
Like ⁴ _____
and some ⁵ _____.

Some live in water,
In oceans, seas and lakes.

**Amazing, amazing animals
What can animals do?
They can fly, they can swim, they can jump!
We share the earth with you!**

4 Answer the questions.

1 Where do bears live?

_____

2 Where do fish live?

_____

3 Where do toucans live?

_____

4 Where do camels live?

_____

Story

5 **Read. Then write can or can't.**

At the Zoo

Luke and Amy are at the zoo. They watch a sea lion show. The sea lion can clap to music. It can't sing very well so Luke covers his ears. The sea lion can balance a ball. It can do lots of tricks. Luke and Amy go to the parrot show. The parrot can ride a bike. It can say its name. It can talk! The parrot can't stop talking.

1 The sea lion _____ clap to music.

2 The sea lion _____ sing well.

3 The sea lion _____ do tricks.

4 The parrot _____ ride a bike.

5 The parrot _____ say its name.

6 The parrot _____ stop talking.

6 **Write about what you can do.**

> balance a ball on your nose   clap to music   ride a bike   sing well

I can _____.

I can't _____.

THINK BIG

> do tricks   fly
> jump   swim
> talk   walk

Sea lions can _____.

They can't _____.

Parrots _____.

_____

74

7 Listen and stick. Then number.

a

b

c

d

☐ ☐ ☐ ☐

8 Look and complete the sentences. Use **can** or **can't**.

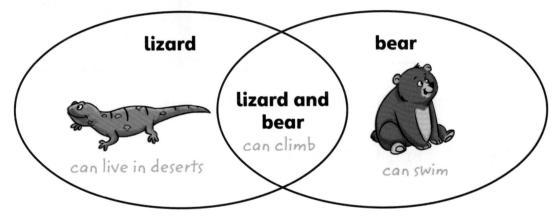

lizard

lizard and bear

can climb

bear

can live in deserts

can swim

1 Lizards and bears _____.

2 Lizards _____ but bears _____.

3 Bears _____ but lizards _____.

9 Read and circle.

1 Can **a camel / camels** live in deserts?
Yes, it can.

2 Can **a lizard / lizards** climb? Yes, they can.

3 Can **bears / a bear** fly? No, they can't.

4 Can **a shark / sharks** walk? No, it can't.

10 **Answer the questions.**

1 Can a bear climb?

_____

2 Can penguins fly?

_____

3 Can a shark sing?

_____

4 Can lizards talk?

_____

5 Can sea lions do tricks?

_____

11 **Look and complete. Use the words from the box.**

| can | can't | fly | swim | they |

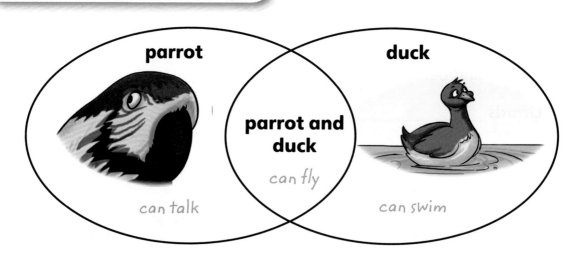

parrot

duck

parrot and duck

can fly

can talk

can swim

Parrots and ducks can ¹ _____. Parrots ² _____ talk
but ³ _____ can't swim. Ducks can ⁴ _____ but they
⁵ _____ talk.

12 **Look and write.**

| chameleon | grey tree frog | polar bear | stonefish |

1 _____

2 _____

3 _____

4 _____

77

13 **Read and circle. Then listen and check.**

1   The polar bear lives on the ice and ¹ **snow / rocks** of the polar regions. Everywhere is white, so its white fur blends in with its surroundings. Polar bears can run ² **fast / slowly** and they can swim, too, which makes them great hunters in the sea as well as on the ice and snow.

2   In rainforests and in deserts, the ³ **shape / colour** of the surroundings isn't always the same. The chameleon's camouflage is very clever because it can change its colour to ⁴ **blend in / hunt fish**. When it's in a ⁵ **tree / desert**, it's green. When it's on a rock, it's brown or grey.

3   Stonefish live in the ocean. They like to eat fish, so they sit on the bottom of the ⁶ **sea / tree** and wait. They look like stones, so the fish can't see them. If a fish touches it, the stonefish stings it and kills it. Then it eats the fish.

4   In the forests of North America, there are grey tree frogs. Birds and ⁷ **polar bears / snakes** like to eat them, but they look like tree branches! Their camouflage helps them to ⁸ **hunt / hide**.

14 Read and match.

1 A polar bear

2 A chameleon

3 A stonefish

4 A grey tree frog

a waits at the bottom of the sea and kills fish with its sting.

b can camouflage by changing its colour.

c can hide from danger because it looks like branches in the forest.

d is difficult to see because all its fur is white.

15 Look at 13. Circle T for true and F for false.

1 The polar bear changes the colour of its fur to blend in. T F

2 Polar bears are great hunters. T F

3 The chameleon changes the colour of its surroundings. T F

4 The stonefish can eat stones. T F

5 Grey tree frogs look like snakes. T F

6 Grey tree frogs can live in trees. T F

 THINK BIG

Complete and colour.

1 A chameleon on a brown rock is _____.

2 A chameleon on a green branch is _____.

16 **Complete the table.**

quiet	quietly
slow	1 _____
easy	easily
2 _____	carefully
good	3 _____
fast	fast
hard	4 _____
far	5 _____
6 _____	badly

17 **Read and ✓ the correct sentences.**

1   Camels can walk very far. ☐

2   Kangaroos jump very well. ☐

3   A crocodile's skin is very hardly. ☐

4   Monkeys can climb good. ☐

5   Sea lions are good swimmers. ☐

6   This bird sings so beautiful. ☐

7   Bats listen carefully. ☐

8   Polar bears run very fastly. ☐

18 **Look at 17. Correct the wrong sentences.**

1   _____

2   _____

3   _____

4   _____

19 Read and circle.

1   My parrot is so **noisy / noisily**.

Our dog eats **noisy / noisily**.

2   You have to be **quiet / quietly** in the library.

Please read **quiet / quietly**!

3   Snakes move **quick / quickly** to catch food.

It's a **quick / quickly** walk to the pet shop.

4   This computer is very **slow / slowly**.

The camel walked **slow / slowly** across the hot desert.

5   The English test is **easy / easily**.

I can **easy / easily** do my homework.

6   She speaks English very **good / well**.

The new Captain America movie is very **good / well**.

7   Look at this! I draw very **bad / badly**!

Look at this! It's a very **bad / badly** drawing!

20 Read and write.

> carefully   far   good   hard   quietly   well

1   The shopping centre isn't very _____.

2   If you look _____, you'll see the deer behind the tree.

3   You have to speak _____ in the library.

4   Speak up! I can't hear you very _____.

5   This film is very _____.

6   I must study _____ for this test.

21 **Look and write.**

canary   cat   dog   lizard   snake

1 _____   2 _____   3 _____

4 _____   5 _____

80
22 **Read and write. Use your answers in 21. Then listen and check.**

1   Pets are good company and relax us when we play with them. They can also be helpful. When we walk our ¹ _____, we keep fit. They can keep us safe, too, and cats keep mice and insects away.

2   In China, people like to have a ² _____ as a pet, and the Chinese believe that they bring good luck to a home. In the U.S.A. there are about 93 million of them!

3   Birds are popular pets, too. In Mexico, the parakeet is a favourite bird. Parakeets can talk and they like playing! In Italy, the ³ _____ is a popular pet bird. These birds sing beautifully!

4   There are dangerous pets, too. You can have a tarantula! When they bite, it's very painful, but they're usually quiet and don't bite. Some people have a pet ⁴ _____ or alligator, so the owner has to be very careful. There are millions of owners of pet reptiles around the world. A gecko, an iguana or a ⁵ _____ can be interesting to keep. They're exotic and not dangerous.

5   We all like different pets for different reasons. The important thing is to look after your pet and to love it as part of your family.

23 **Look at 22. Read and match.**

1 Pets are good to have because

2 Cats are popular in China because

3 The canary is a popular bird because

4 Be careful with your tarantula because

5 A lizard can be a good pet because

a it's exotic and interesting but not dangerous.

b it sings beautifully.

c it might give you a painful bite.

d they relax us and can be helpful.

e people believe they bring good luck.

24 **Put the words in order.**

1 | all | different | like | pets. | We |

_____

2 | have | dangerous | Some | people | pets. |

_____

3 | must | You | pet. | love and | your | look after |

_____

4 | insects | Cats | our houses. | keep | from | mice and | away |

_____

5 | U.S.A. | pet cats | the | about | 93 million | in | are | There |

_____

Read and write about you.

THINK BIG

My name is _____. I live in _____.

_____ are popular pets here. They can

_____ and _____. They can't

_____ or _____.

25 **Read. Circle the best topic sentence for the main idea.**

1 Main idea: Polar bears are my favourite animal.

   a Polar bears live in cold places.

   b Some days are cold in the winter.

   c I like polar bears.

2 Main idea: It's important to take care of pets.

   a I want a pet parakeet.

   b I feed my cat every day.

   c People all over the world have got pets.

3 Main idea: Some animals can change colour.

   a Some animals can look like different things.

   b Some animals are not good pets.

   c Some animals can do tricks.

4 Main idea: Zoos are great places.

   a A parrot can talk.

   b I always have fun at the zoo.

   c Dogs are fun pets.

26 **Write a topic sentence for the following titles.**

1 My Favourite Animal

_____

2 My Favourite Time of Day

_____

3 An Unusual Job

_____

27 **Read and circle ea, oi and oe.**

eat

Spain

boil

bean

meat

toe

oil

joy

28 **Underline the words with ea, oi and oe. Then read aloud.**

1 Joe likes boiled beans with oil.

2 I eat meat and drink tea.

29 **Connect the letters. Then write.**

1 p   oil   **a** _ _ _ _

2 b   oe   **b** _ _ _

3 t   each   **c** _ _ _ _ _

86

30 **Listen and write.**

So, Joe, boil the ¹_____,

Add the ²_____,

Add the ³_____.

Eat the ⁴_____,

Eat the meat,

Eat the ⁵_____

And drink the ⁶_____.

31 **Read and answer.**

1 Can snakes eat sharks? _____

2 Can a bear climb? _____

3 Can a lizard sing? _____

4 Can parrots talk? _____

32 **Think about the animals you know. Complete the chart.**

These animals can swim.	These animals can fly.	These animals can climb trees.
1	1	1
2	2	2
3	3	3
4	4	4

33 **Match the questions and answers.**

1 What can toucans do?

2 What can you do?

3 Can an owl jump?

4 Can a shark swim?

5 What can a parrot do?

6 Can deer jump and run?

a Yes, it can.

b They can fly.

c Yes, they can.

d No, it can't but it can fly.

e I can swim, run and talk.

f It can fly but it can't swim.

34 **Correct the sentences.**

1 Sea lions can swim good. _____

2 Canaries sing beautiful. _____

3 Sea lions sing bad. _____

4 A chameleon can change colour easy. _____

unit 5

Wonderful Weather!

1 🗨 **Match.**

1

2

3

4

5

6

 a It's hot and sunny.

 b It's windy.

 c It's cool and cloudy.

 d It's cold and snowy.

 e It's rainy.

 f It's warm.

2 🗨 **What's the weather like today?**

It's _____.

It isn't _____.

3 **Listen and circle the five incorrect words. Then listen and write.**

Cool Weekend!

What's the weather like today?
Rainy, windy, hot or cold?

On Sunday, it was rainy,
It was very hot, too.
I was nice and cool in my winter coat,
Outside the sky wasn't blue!

Now, it's Tuesday. It's sunny.
Great! I can go out and play.
Oh, no! I have to go to school.
Never mind! The weekend was cold!

Chorus (x2)

1 _____

2 _____

3 _____

4 _____

5 _____

4 **Look at 1. Complete the sentences. Use words from the box.**

coat   scarf   shorts   sunglasses   T-shirt

1 On hot and sunny days, Jim wears _____.

2 On warm days, Iris wears a _____.

3 On cloudy and cool days, Dan wears a _____.

4 On warm rainy days, Maria wears _____ and boots.

5 On cold and snowy days, Joe wears a _____.

5 **What was the weather like yesterday? Draw and write.**

It was _____. It wasn't _____.

6 Read and ✓.

Amy is Ready!

Amy is going on a hike. It was rainy yesterday. Amy's mum doesn't want her to get wet today so Amy gets a raincoat and an umbrella. It was cold and windy yesterday. Amy's mum doesn't want her to get cold so she gets her jumper, her hat and gloves. It's sunny today. Amy's mum gives her sunscreen and sunglasses. Now Amy's ready!

1 It was rainy yesterday. Amy gets

☐ sunglasses.   ☐ an umbrella.   ☐ a jumper.   ☐ a raincoat.

2 It was cold and windy yesterday. Amy gets

☐ a jumper.   ☐ sandals.   ☐ shorts.   ☐ gloves.

3 It's warm and sunny now. Amy's mum gives her

☐ boots.   ☐ a coat.   ☐ sunscreen.   ☐ sunglasses.

7 Read and write.

cloudy   cold   cool   hot   rainy   snowy

1 What's the weather like today? It's _____.

2 What was the weather like yesterday? It was _____.

THINK BIG Draw and write.

HOT

COLD

I wear _____ on sunny days.

I wear _____ on cold days.

95
8 Listen and stick.

San Francisco	
Yesterday	Today

Puerto Rico	
Yesterday	Today

9 What was the weather like? Match and write.

1 On Monday, _____.

2 _____

3 _____

4 _____

5 _____

Language in Action

10 **Read and look. Circle T for true and F for false.**

Yesterday	Today

1	Yesterday, the weather was cool.	T	F
2	It wasn't windy yesterday.	T	F
3	It's cloudy today.	T	F
4	It's cold today.	T	F
5	It was sunny yesterday.	T	F
6	It's cool and sunny today.	T	F

11 **Look at 10. Write the answers.**

1 What was the weather like yesterday? _____

2 What's the weather like today? _____

12 **Write about you.**

1 What was the weather like yesterday? _____

13 **Read and make sentences.**

1 I / ✗ / hot / yesterday

_____

2 We / ✗ / cool / last weekend

_____

3 It / ✓ / sunny / now

_____

4 It / ✗ / windy / today

_____

14 What's the weather like? Look and write.

1 _____

2 _____

3 _____

4 _____

5 _____

97

15 Read and write. Then listen and check your answers.

| climate | extreme | moon | opposite | seasons | temperature |

1   The weather in a place is called the ¹ _____. Different places on the planet have different climates, and these change with the ² _____. In some places, like Southern Europe, winters are mild and it's often rainy with not much snow. But in other places, the climate is extreme – the weather is very hot, very cold or there's a lot of rain.

2   In the Lut Desert in Iran, for example, it's very hot and dry. The ³ _____ can reach 70 degrees Celsius. This is why there's no life there in some parts – and no tourists! However, lots of tourists visit the Atacama Desert in Chile. It's also dry there but temperatures are milder. Atacama looks like the surface of the ⁴ _____ – it almost never rains there. On the other hand, it rains almost every day in Lloró, Colombia. Trees grow quickly there because it's so wet.

3   If you like very cold temperatures, you can visit a place like Oymyakon, Russia. It's the ⁵ _____ of a place like Lut Desert. The winters there are ⁶ _____, with temperatures as low as -70 degrees Celsius. There's a lot of snow and ice, and schools only close if the temperature is below -52 degrees Celsius!

16 Look at 15 and match.

1 Atacama Desert, Chile

2 Oymyakon, Russia

3 Lloró, Colombia

4 Lut Desert, Iran

a

b

c

d

17 Look at 15. Read and match.

1 Not many people go to the Lut Desert.   a because of the cold climate.
2 The Atacama desert is very dry   b As a result, the trees grow quickly.
3 It rains a lot in Lloró, Colombia.   c As a result, it's a quiet place.
4 Not many people live in Oymyakon   d because it never rains.

18 Look at 15. Read and write.

1 It snows a lot in _____, _____.
2 The _____ Desert in _____ is dry and looks like the moon.
3 It's very wet in _____, _____.
4 It's too hot to live in the _____ _____, Iran.

Find the odd one out.

THINK
BIG

1 Lloró   2 Atacama Desert
3 Lut Desert   4 Oymyakon, Russia

The odd one out is _____

because _____.

19 **Look and write. Use was or wasn't.**

M	T	W	Th	F

1 Last Monday, it _____ sunny.

2 Last Tuesday, it _____ rainy.

3 Last Wednesday, it _____ cloudy.

4 Last Thursday, it _____ windy.

5 Last Friday, it _____ snowy.

20 **Read and circle.**

1 There **was / were** a lot of rain.

2 There **was / were** boats on the river.

3 There **was / were** sharks in the water.

4 There **was / were** children in the park.

5 There **was / were** a kite in the sky.

6 There **was / were** a snowman in the road!

21 **Look at 20. Make negative sentences.**

1 _____

2 _____

3 _____

4 _____

5 _____

6 _____

22 **Read and write. Use was, were or weren't.**

Danny and Leo ¹ _____ lost in the forest and
it ² _____ late. Then there ³ _____
a noise. ⁴ _____ it an owl? ⁵ _____
there bears here? The boys ⁶ _____ sure. Leo
⁷ _____ scared. He ⁸ _____ cold
and he ⁹ _____ hungry. "Look!" said Danny.
There ¹⁰ _____ a house. The lights
¹¹ _____ on. "Come on!" he said. There
¹² _____ nice people in the house. Danny and
Leo ¹³ _____ happy.

23 **Read the answers and write questions.**

1 He was in New York last year.
Where _____?

2 She was in bed at 9 p.m. last night.
When _____?

3 Her aunt was in the hospital.
Where _____?

4 They were at our house last weekend.
When _____?

5 John was with Eric's parents.
Who _____?

6 Mary and Anna were at the shops this morning.
Where _____?

7 They were at work at 7 a.m. yesterday morning.
What time _____?

99

24 **Read and circle. Then listen and check your answers.**

1 **¹ Sports / exams** are fun for children everywhere. Baseball and basketball are very popular in the U.S.A. Cricket and field hockey are favourite sports in India and England. Football is popular everywhere. Kids love to be **² active / asleep**.

2 If the **³ weather / television** is bad, you can still have **⁴ fun / chores**. When it's windy, you can fly a kite. In some Asian countries, like Japan, children love flying kites. Some like to make their own kites – and you can try this, too! Just look on the Internet for ideas.

3 For much of the year, parts of Africa are very dry. When lots of **⁵ rain / weather** comes, the lakes and rivers fill up and children can go swimming and **⁶ play / work** in the water.

4 Snow is fun, too, of course. You can go **⁷ skiing / swimming** or sledging or you can make **⁸ dinner / snowmen**. You can have snowball fights as well. In places with a lot of snow, such as Canada and Alaska, some kids go dog sledging. Dogs pull sledges in the snow and the kids ride on them.

5 So, when the weather is bad, don't stay **⁹ at school / inside**. Put on the right clothes or get an umbrella, and go **¹⁰ to bed / outside**!

25 **Which paragraph? Look at 24 and match paragraphs 1–5 to pictures a–e.**

a

b

c

d

e

26 **Read and match.**

1 Some children fly kites   **a** on rainy days.

2 Some children in Africa go swimming   **b** on cold and snowy days.

3 Some children go dog sledging   **c** on windy days.

27 **Put the words in order.**

1 | active. | love | be | Kids | to |

_____

2 | windy, | a kite. | you | can | it's | When | fly |

_____

3 | rains. | when | Africa, | In | children | it | swim |

_____

4 | make | snowy. | You | it's | can | snowmen | when |

_____

5 | snow. | the | in | pull | Dogs | sledges |

_____

Do you like these sports? Write numbers to rate them.

THINK BIG

1 = I love it!   2 = I like it.   3 = I don't like it.

_____ flying kites   _____ riding a bike

_____ playing volleyball   _____ swimming

_____ doing gymnastics   _____ playing football

_____ sledging   _____ running

_____ playing baseball

28 **Read. Number the detail sentences 1 or 2 to go with topic sentence 1 or 2.**

Topic sentence 1: *I like hot, sunny weather.*

Topic sentence 2: *My best friend is Julie.*

☐

a I swim in the sea on hot days.

☐

b Julie is in my class at school.

☐

c She wants to be a firefighter.

☐

d We play football together after school.

☐

e I like riding my bike in the sun.

☐

f I want to go to a desert.

29 **Write the best detail sentence to start each paragraph. Choose from the box.**

Cats were everywhere!   I take care of my pet every day.   Maths is fun.

1 Topic sentence: I've got a pet.

Detail sentences: My pet's name is Tiny. He is a very small fish. He loves swimming every day.

_____

_____

2 Topic sentence: Maths is my favourite subject.

Detail sentences: Maths is easy for me. I help my friends with it.

_____

_____

30 **Read and circle sc, sw, sn and sl.**

snail   snow   scout

coin   slow

sweet   swim   foe

scarf   sleep

31 **Underline the words with sc, sw, sn and sl. Then read aloud.**

1 There is a swan sleeping on the swing.

2 Put on your scarf and put on your skiis. It's snowing!

32 **Connect the letters. Then write.**

1 sl   ail   **a** _ _ _ _ _

2 sn   arf   **b** _ _ _ _ _

3 sw   eep   **c** _ _ _ _ _

4 sc   eet   **d** _ _ _ _ _

104

 33 **Listen and write.**

A ¹ _____

² _____ is eating

A ³ _____

And a ⁴ _____

⁵ _____ is swimming.

34 **Read and choose.**

1 It's hot and dry there **because** / **so** it never rains.

2 **As** / **So** a result, few people live there.

3 The trees grow quickly because **of** / **to** the rainy climate.

4 **No** / **Not** many trees grow there because it's so hot.

5 Not many people live there **because of** / **few** the extreme temperature.

35 **Read and complete with is, isn't, was and wasn't.**

Emily: Hi, Sam. It ¹ _____ fun to see you yesterday.

Sam: Yes, I had fun, too.

Emily: What ² _____ the weather like this afternoon?

Sam: It was cool this morning but it ³ _____ hot now.

Emily: It's the same here! It ⁴ _____ hot this morning but it's hot now.

Sam: That's funny. I'm happy it ⁵ _____ rainy. I don't like the rain.

Emily: I love the rain. I can watch TV!

Smells Good!

1 **Complete the sentences. Use words from the box.**

| feels | looks | smell | sounds | tastes |

1 My jumper _____ soft.

2 This pie _____ delicious.

3 This music _____ amazing.

4 My hair _____ terrible.

5 These flowers _____ nice.

2 **Write about you.**

1 What smells awful? _____

2 What smells wonderful? _____

3 **Listen and number in order.**

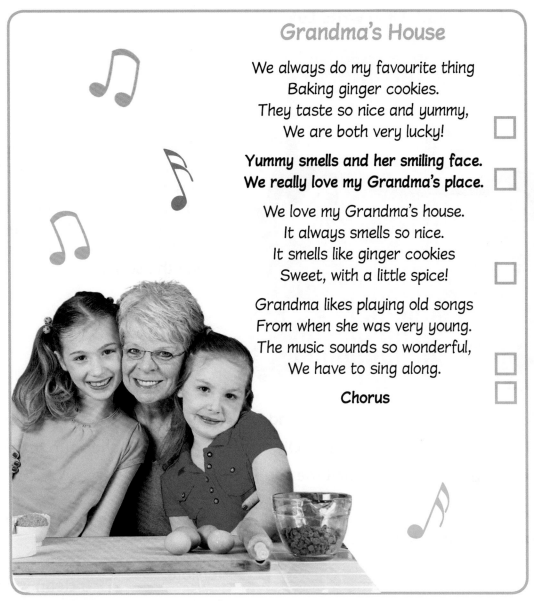

Grandma's House

We always do my favourite thing
Baking ginger cookies.
They taste so nice and yummy,
We are both very lucky! ☐

Yummy smells and her smiling face.
We really love my Grandma's place. ☐

We love my Grandma's house.
It always smells so nice.
It smells like ginger cookies
Sweet, with a little spice! ☐

Grandma likes playing old songs
From when she was very young.
The music sounds so wonderful,
We have to sing along. ☐

Chorus ☐

4 **Look and read. Then circle.**

1 How does the apple taste? It tastes **delicious** / **bad**.

2 How do these shoes feel? They feel **soft** / **tight**.

3 How does my hair look? It looks **terrible** / **nice**.

4 How does the band sound? The band sounds **bad** / **good**.

5 How do the flowers smell? They smell **awful** / **sweet**.

5 Look and read. Then write Luke or Amy.

It Tastes Terrible!

Luke smells the fish soup. He thinks it smells horrible. He thinks the soup looks bad, too. Amy tastes the soup and says, "It tastes... OK." Luke tries the soup. He says, "It tastes terrible." Amy has got a cold. She can't smell or taste the soup.

1 _____ thinks the soup smells bad.

2 _____ thinks the soup doesn't look good.

3 _____ thinks the soup tastes OK.

4 _____ thinks the soup tastes terrible.

5 _____ can't taste or smell the soup.

6 Think and write about you. Use smell or taste and the words from the box or your own ideas.

I think _____ terrible.

I think _____ nice.

I think _____ horrible.

I think _____ delicious.

a clean sock
a flower   chocolate
fish soup   ice cream

THINK BIG Put in order.

awful   bad   good   great   OK

_____ very bad _____ _____ _____ very good _____

114

7 Listen and stick. Then number.

a ☐

b ☐

c ☐

d ☐

8 Read and circle. Then complete. Use the words from the box.

> delicious   nice   quiet   soft   tight

1 I'm wearing my new shoes.

They **taste / feel** _____.

2 My baby brother isn't crying.

The house **tastes / sounds** _____.

3 I'm taking a walk in the garden.

The flowers **smell / sound** _____.

4 I'm eating my favourite lunch.

It **feels / tastes** _____.

5 You're wearing my new jumper.

It **looks / sounds** _____.

9 **Circle the correct word.**

1 How **do / does** the soup taste?   2 How **do / does** the pizza taste?

3 How **do / does** the sandals feel?   4 How **do / does** the apples smell?

5 How **do / does** the music sound?   6 How **do / does** the shirts look?

10 **Complete the questions. Then look and complete the answers.**

1 **A:** How _____ the sand feel?   2 **A:** How _____ the hat look?

   B: It _____ hot.   **B:** It _____ pretty.

3 **A:** How _____ the birds sound?   4 **A:** How _____ the sandwiches taste?

   B: They _____ loud.   **B:** They _____ delicious.

11 **Draw an interesting or funny cake. Colour. Then write.**

1 How does it taste?

_____

2 How does it smell?

_____

3 How does it look?

_____

12 **Find and write the words.**

ensak

1 _____

haleoncem

2 _____

yutbferlt

3 _____

tab

4 _____

116
13 **Listen, read and write.**

> brain   danger   echo   hear   senses   smell
> sound waves   taste buds   tastes   tongues

1   Our ¹ _____ are sending information to our ² _____ all the time. We need this information to know where we are and to understand the world around us.

2   Our senses keep us safe. For example, we can feel if something is hot or sharp. We can see and ³ _____ if we're in ⁴ _____. When we need food, our senses tell us if our food looks, smells and ⁵ _____ good. Then we can decide if it's a good idea to eat it.

3   Animals have senses, too. They're very different from people's senses. We see with our eyes but bats can't see well so they use their ears. They make sounds and listen for an ⁶ _____. The ⁷ _____ of the echo tell them where something is and its size.

4   Reptiles like snakes, lizards and chameleons ⁸ _____ with their ⁹ _____ and not with their noses. They taste the air. Butterflies have got tiny ¹⁰ _____ on their feet. They tell the butterfly what flower it's on. Then they know if they can eat it.

14 **Look at 13. Use the clues to complete the crossword puzzle.**

Across →

1 Snakes _____ with their tongues.

2 Butterflies _____ with their legs.

3 Our _____ keep us safe.

Down ↓

1 Bats use their ears to _____ things.

2 Chameleons use their _____ to catch food.

15 **Read and match.**

1 We understand the world around us

2 We can taste food and look at it

3 Animals use their senses, too,

4 A bat can see in the dark because

5 Reptiles taste the air around them

a it makes sounds and listens carefully.

b but they often use them differently.

c to know where there is food or danger.

d to know if it's good to eat.

e because our senses send information to our brain.

Which animals use these senses? Match.

THINK
BIG

a shark

b elephant

c tarsier

1 Because of its large ears, it's got a very good sense of hearing. It also uses its trunk and feet to hear.

2 It uses its big eyes to find food at night.

3 It's got a good sense of smell. It can smell food in the water from far away.

16 **Circle. Then write the answer.**

1

How **do / does** my hair look?

(It/great) _____.

2

How **do / does** the band sound?

(It/awful) _____.

3

How **do / does** the apple taste?

(It/lovely) _____.

4

How **do / does** your shoes feel?

(They/tight) _____.

5

How **do / does** your jumper feel?

(It/soft) _____.

6

How **do / does** the flowers smell?

(They/nice) _____.

17 **Read and write the answers.**

1 Does it sound OK? No, _____.

2 Do they look nice? No, _____.

3 Does it taste spicy? No, _____.

4 Does it sound like a violin? Yes, _____.

5 Does it feel soft? No, _____.

6 Do they taste salty? Yes, _____.

7 Does it smell like lemon? Yes, _____.

Grammar

18 **Write questions with How.**

1 your new MP3 player/sound

_____

2 my dress/look

_____

3 the jeans/feel

_____

4 the soup/taste

_____

5 her perfume/smell

_____

19 **Read and match.**

1 I have to wear a uniform.   **a** It smells awful!

2 I got a jazz CD.   **b** It tastes delicious.

3 Try the ice cream.   **c** It feels tight.

4 I didn't take out the rubbish.   **d** It looks good.

5 We painted his bedroom.   **e** It sounds great!

20 **Put the words in order.**

1 | plays | every night. | in her room | She | her guitar |

_____

2 | a strange smell | in the garage | There | all the time. | is |

_____

3 | in the kitchen | tasted | before dinner. | the soup | He |

_____

4 | at 12:30 p.m. | at school | We always | a break for lunch | have |

_____

5 | in Spain | visit | every year. | They | their cousins |

_____

21 **Look, read and match.**

1 rubbish collector

2 zoo keeper

3 baker

4 flower seller

119
22 **Read and write. Then listen and check.**

| after | awful | bath | colours | fresh | sneeze | stinks | treats |

1   André Tyrode is from Lyon. He makes cakes and pastries every day. He says everything he makes tastes and smells wonderful. He hates getting up early but he loves the smell of [1] _____ bread. It makes him happy to make nice [2] _____ for people to eat.

2   Alberto Rivera is from Costa Rica and he grows and sells flowers on his farm. He sends them all over the world. He loves to smell the flowers and he likes their different [3] _____. Sometimes the flowers make him [4] _____. Flowers are beautiful and they help him remember that the world is beautiful.

3   Candace Reilly is from Calgary in Canada. Her job is to pick up rubbish and help keep her city clean. It's a very important job but the smell can be terrible. She says the rubbish really [5] _____ sometimes but she's happy to make her city look better. She really likes her job.

4   Sarah Ang is from Singapore. She works at Singapore Zoo and looks [6] _____ one of the largest Asian elephants in the world – Zelda. She often has to give her a [7] _____ and she gets wet, too. She says the smell can be [8] _____ but she likes looking after her.

23 **Find and write the words.**

ekasc

losfewr

satipers

1 _____

2 _____

3 _____

walfu

nktiss

ibsrubh

4 _____

5 _____

6 _____

atbh

eesnez

ayerl

7 _____

8 _____

9 _____

24 **Look at 22. Match and write.**

1 André makes

2 Alberto grows

3 Candace picks up

4 Sarah washes

a flowers. They look _____.

b rubbish. It really _____.

c Zelda the elephant. Zelda smells
   _____.

d pastries. They taste _____.

Do you like these jobs? Write numbers to rate them.

1 = I love it!   2 = I like it.   3 = I don't like it.

_____ Pick up rubbish.   _____ Grow and sell flowers.

_____ Make pastries.   _____ Work at a zoo.

25 **Read and circle T for true and F for false.**

1 A paragraph starts with a final sentence.   T   F

2 A topic sentence is the first sentence in a paragraph.   T   F

3 There are usually a few detail sentences in a paragraph.   T   F

4 A paragraph finishes with a title.   T   F

26 **Read. Match the final sentence to each paragraph.**

1 My favourite animals are sea lions. They sound funny. They can do great tricks and can swim.

2 Butterflies are interesting. They look beautiful and they can fly. They taste with their legs!

3 My grandma's house smells good. Her biscuits taste delicious. She plays the piano. The music sounds wonderful.

a They are my favourite insects!

b It's a great place to visit.

c They are wonderful animals.

27 **Write a final sentence.**

topic sentence → Lizards are amazing.

detail sentences →
Lizards can run fast.
Lizards smell with their tongues.
Lizards usually feel dry and cool.

final sentence → _____

_____

28 **Read and circle fl, pl, gl and bl.**

play   swan   slim

flag   glad   block

flip-flops   glass

plum   black

29 **Underline the words with fl, pl, gl and bl. Then read aloud.**

1 There is a castle with a black flag.

2 Drink the glass of orange juice and eat the plum cake.

30 **Connect the letters. Then write.**

1 fl   um   **a** _ _ _ _

2 pl   ack   **b** _ _ _ _ _

3 gl   ag   **c** _ _ _ _

4 bl   ass   **d** _ _ _ _ _

124

31 **Listen and write.**

It's summer.
Yellow ¹ _____,
Green ² _____.
³
_____,
⁴
_____ shorts,
It's summer.
I'm ⁵ _____!

32 **Look and write.**

1 It _____ delicious.

2 They _____ good.

3 It _____ hot.

4 She _____ beautiful.

5 They _____ loud.

33 **Complete the questions and answer for you.**

1 _____ your hair look today?

_____

2 _____ new clothes feel?

_____

3 _____ a butterfly look?

_____

4 _____ your shoes feel?

_____

My hair looks bad today.

Max's Day at the Zoo

1 **Look at the paths for Max's day at the zoo. Complete the sentences. Use words from the boxes.**

ANIMALS
a camel
a shark
an owl

SENSES
feels
looks
sounds
tastes

START

Max

2 **Look at the paths again. What do you think? Write the answers.**

1 Animal Quiz

It doesn't live in oceans.

It lives in deserts.

It can't fly but it can run fast.

What is it?

_____

2 What was the weather like?

Before the zoo, _____.

After the zoo, _____.

3 **Choose one path. Draw the path. Learn about Max's day at the zoo.**

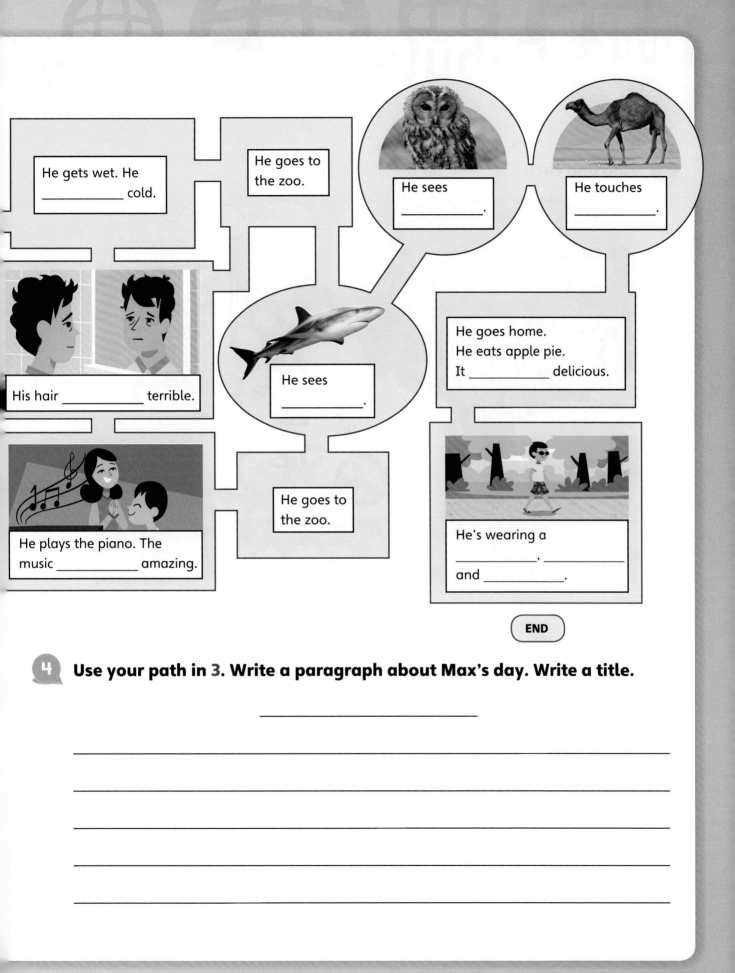

He gets wet. He _____ cold.

He goes to the zoo.

He sees _____.

He touches _____.

His hair _____ terrible.

He sees _____.

He goes home.
He eats apple pie.
It _____ delicious.

He plays the piano. The music _____ amazing.

He goes to the zoo.

He's wearing a _____, _____ and _____.

END

4 Use your path in **3**. Write a paragraph about Max's day. Write a title.

_____

_____

_____

_____

_____

_____

unit 7 Fabulous Food!

1 **Find and circle.**

1	bread	**2**	cheese	**3**	green pepper	**4**	lettuce
5	mushroom	**6**	onions	**7**	cucumbers	**8**	pizza
9	tomatoes						

2 **Draw your favourite food and write.**

Breakfast   Lunch   Dinner

For breakfast, I like eating _____

_____.

3 Listen and circle the five incorrect words. Then listen and write.

I'm Hungry!

Hi, Mum, I'm home from school.
I'm really hungry now.
I'd like to make a burger,
Can you show me how?

1 _____

I am home from my school day.
I'd like a sandwich. Is that OK?

Are there any onions?
Here are some on the shelf.
Is there any mustard?
I see it for myself.

2 _____

3 _____

Chorus

There's just one problem, Mum
There isn't any lettuce!
But I've got a great idea:
Let's have cake instead!

4 _____

5 _____

Chorus

4 Find and write. Then complete for you.

1 reneg speerpp **2** zizap

_____ _____ _____

3 rushmooms **4** atootm cause

_____ _____ _____

I like _____ and _____.

I don't like _____ or _____.

5 **Read and write. Use the words from the box.**

A Surprise for Mum

Amy and Luke want to make dinner. It's a surprise for their mum. There's a green pepper, some cheese and some olives. The cheese and olives are yummy so Luke and Amy eat them. They take some more food out of the fridge. Mum comes home. The surprise isn't dinner. The surprise is a messy kitchen!

1 Amy and Luke are making _____ for their mum.

2 Amy and Luke eat the cheese and _____.

3 Amy and Luke find some more _____ in the fridge.

4 Their _____ isn't happy when she comes home.

5 Mum's surprise is a _____ kitchen.

dinner
food
messy
mum
olives

6 **Look at the story picture in 5. Read and circle the correct answer.**

1 Is there a pineapple on the table?   **Yes, there is. / No, there isn't.**

2 Are there any mushrooms?   **Yes, there are. / No, there aren't.**

3 Is there any cheese?   **Yes, there is. / No, there isn't.**

4 Are there any olives on the table?   **Yes, there are. / No, there aren't.**

THINK BIG **What do you need to make a cake? Find out and ✓.**

eggs ☐   butter ☐   cheese ☐   mushrooms ☐

sugar ☐   flour ☐   onions ☐   strawberries ☐

135

7 **Listen and stick. Then listen and write the food.**

1 _____

2 _____

3 _____

4 _____

8 **Look and circle.**

1 There **are some / aren't any** mushrooms.

2 There **is some / isn't any** mustard.

3 There **is some / isn't any** bread.

4 There **are some / aren't any** cucumbers.

5 There **is some / isn't any** lettuce.

6 There **are some / aren't any** green peppers.

9 **Look and answer. Use some or any.**

1 Is there any milk? _____

2 Is there any turkey? _____

3 Is there any tomato sauce? _____

4 Are there any eggs? _____

5 Are there any red peppers? _____

10 **Look at 9. Write the questions.**

1 _____ Yes, there is some cheese.

2 _____ Yes, there is some mustard.

3 _____ No, there aren't any onions.

4 _____ Yes, there are some green peppers.

5 _____ No, there isn't any juice.

11 **Read. Then write A, B, C, D or E.**

	Where do we get the vitamins in food?
Vitamin A	carrots, mangoes, milk, eggs
Vitamin B	potatoes, bread, chicken, cheese, eggs, green vegetables
Vitamin C	oranges, peppers, tomatoes, potatoes
Vitamin D	eggs, fish, milk, the sun
Vitamin E	nuts, green vegetables

1 Vitamin ____   **2** Vitamin ____, ____ and ____   **3** Vitamin ____

4 Vitamin ____   **5** Vitamin ____ and ____   **6** Vitamin ____

 138

12 **Listen, read and write.**

energy   good   healthy   important
naturally   strong   treats

1   Vitamins are very ¹ _____ for our bodies to stay ² _____ and healthy. Vitamins are in food and drink. You need to have vitamins every day. Vitamins A, D and E live in the fat in our bodies. Vitamins C and B live in the water in our bodies.

2   Vitamin A is good for your eyes and skin. It's in orange and yellow fruits. Vitamin D makes our bones strong. Our body makes Vitamin D ³ _____ when it's in the sun. Vitamin E in nuts and green vegetables keeps your blood ⁴ _____. Vitamin C is ⁵ _____ for our bones, our teeth and our brain.

3   There are different kinds of Vitamin B and they're in different foods. Some kinds give us ⁶ _____ for our muscles. Others help make blood. You can find vitamin B in some ⁷ _____, too, like dark chocolate!

13 **Look at 12. Read and circle.**

1 Vitamin A is good for our **eyes / ears**.

2 Vitamin B helps make blood and gives us **energy / skin**.

3 Vitamin C is good for bones, teeth and our **brain / muscles**.

4 Vitamin D helps make strong **skin / bones**.

5 Vitamin E keeps our **blood / muscles** healthy.

14 **Read and match.**

1 Vitamins are in food and drink and

2 Vitamins are very important if

3 The sun helps our body

4 There are different kinds of Vitamin B

5 Fruit and vegetables are good for you

a make Vitamin D naturally.

b and you should try to have at least five a day.

c live in our body fat or water.

d we are to stay healthy.

e which give us energy or make our blood.

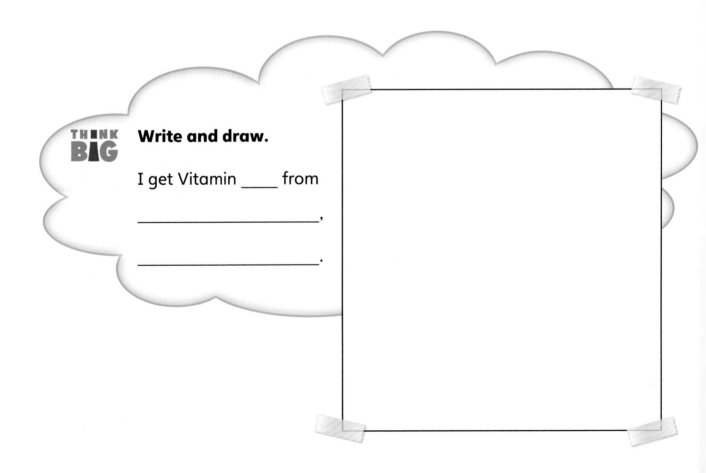

THINK BIG **Write and draw.**

I get Vitamin _____ from

_____,

_____.

15 **Write some, a or an.**

1 I've got _____ peppers.

2 I haven't got _____ onion.

3 I've got_____ milk.

4 I've got _____ ketchup.

5 I haven't got _____ egg.

6 I've got_____ cheese.

7 I haven't got _____ tomato.

8 I haven't got _____ potato.

16 **Read the dialogue and write. Use some, much or many.**

I want to make
1 _____ pancakes.

We don't have
2 _____ eggs.

That's OK, we only need
three. But we don't have
3 _____ milk.

I can get 4 _____
at the shops.

Can you get 5 _____
maple syrup, too?

OK. But don't make too
6 _____ pancakes!

Grammar

17 **Read and circle.**

1 How **much** / **many** pizza do you want?

2 How **much** / **many** money have you got?

3 How **much** / **many** sweets are there?

4 How **much** / **many** ice cream would you like?

5 How **much** / **many** slices of pizza do you want?

6 How **much** / **many** fruit do you eat every day?

18 **Read and ✓.**

1 There's just ☐ a lot of milk in the fridge, so don't use it all.
☐ a little
☐ a few

2 There aren't many sweets in the bag, there are just ☐ a lot of.
☐ a little.
☐ a few.

3 He bought ☐ a lot of souvenirs, and now he's got no money!
☐ a little
☐ a few

4 We've only got ☐ a lot of players for the game on Sunday.
☐ a little
☐ a few

5 I did ☐ a lot of homework this evening, so now I want to have a rest.
☐ a little
☐ a few

19 **Look, read and write the foods.**

beans and toast   churros   huevos rancheros   rice, soup and fish

Mexico   **Australia**   **Japan**   **Spain**

1 _____ **2** _____ **3** _____ **4** _____

141

20 **Listen, read and write. Then check your answers in 19.**

breakfast   cereal   delicious   doughnuts   meal
pickles   sugar   toast   toasted

1   In the U.K., Katie's mum says ¹ _____ is the most important ² _____ of the day. On weekdays, Katie has cereal with milk and banana, boiled eggs with toast and marmite or brown bread soldiers. At the weekend, she usually has bacon and tomato sandwiches. She doesn't like porridge but her mum loves it.

2   Yoko is from Japan and she never eats any ³ _____. In the morning, she usually eats rice, soup, fish and ⁴ _____.

3   Luis, from Spain, likes to eat bread or cereal when he gets up. Sometimes at weekends, he has churros with chocolate. Churros are like little ⁵ _____.

4   In Mexico, Camilla often eats fried eggs for breakfast. In Spanish, they're called huevos rancheros and she puts them on ⁶ _____ tortillas with some salsa. They're spicy, colourful and taste ⁷ _____.

5   Tony in Australia also likes marmite (it's brown and salty and you can put it on your ⁸ _____). He also eats porridge and puts cream and some brown ⁹ _____ on top. He loves eating beans on toast in the morning.

21 **Look at 20. Circle T for true and F for false.**

1 Katie has bacon and marmite sandwiches.   T   F
2 Yoko never eats rice or fish for breakfast.   T   F
3 Luis sometimes eats churros with chocolate.   T   F
4 Camila eats salsa with her huevos rancheros.   T   F
5 Tony has brown sugar on his toast.   T   F

22 **Put the words in order.**

1 | is | breakfast | very | good | A | important. |

_____

2 | porridge, | honey | mum | on | Katie's | likes | her |

_____

3 | usually | rice, | fish. | has | soup | Yoko | and |

_____

4 | has | churros | Luis | sometimes | eats | eggs. | but | usually |

_____

5 | to | toast | beans | likes | on | eat | top. | Tony | with |

_____

Draw a picture of your favourite breakfast and write.

THINK BIG

My favourite breakfast is

_____.

It's important to eat a good breakfast because

_____

_____.

title ⟶ **My Favourite Breakfast**
by Laura Brown

topic sentence ⟶ I like a lot of different things for breakfast but I have my favourite breakfast every Sunday morning.

detail sentences ⟶ I start with some orange slices, cold from the fridge. Then my mother makes two fluffy pancakes for me. I put butter on them and then I put warm maple syrup on top. The pancakes are delicious with a glass of cold milk.

final sentence ⟶ My favourite breakfast makes Sundays special.

23 **Write. Use the words from the box.**

detail sentences   final sentence   title   topic sentence

1 _____ ⟶ Huevos rancheros are the best breakfast food.

2 _____ ⟶ Sunday Morning Breakfast with Huevos Rancheros

3 _____ ⟶ My mum starts with a tortilla. She toasts the tortilla in a pan and then puts the tortilla on a plate. I help her fry some eggs in a pan. Then she puts the eggs on top of the tortilla. I put salsa on the eggs and they taste amazing!

4 _____ ⟶ My mum makes huevos rancheros for breakfast on Sunday mornings.

24 **Look at 23. Write the paragraph in order.**

_____

_____

_____

_____

_____

25 **Read and circle br, cr, dr, fr, gr, pr and tr.**

> **bread** **grass** **dream** **glad**
> **cream** frog plant **prize** **train**

26 **Underline the words with br, cr, dr, fr, gr, pr and tr. Then read aloud.**

1 The frog's driving the green and brown train.

2 She's crying because she's got a prize and she's happy.

27 **Connect the letters. Then write.**

1	br	eam	**a** _ _ _ _ _
2	cr	oll	**b** _ _ _ _ _
3	fr	ead	**c** _ _ _ _ _
4	tr	ass	**d** _ _ _ _ _
5	gr	og	**e** _ _ _ _
6	pr	ive	**f** _ _ _ _ _
7	dr	ize	**g** _ _ _ _ _

147

28 **Listen and write.**

Every night,
I ¹ _____
About a ² _____
And a ³ _____
And a ⁴ _____
⁵ _____!
In my dream,
They eat ⁶ _____
With ⁷ _____.

29 **Look. Then circle the different kinds of food.**

1

The sandwich has got:

bread	green peppers
tomatoes	mustard
turkey	onions
cheese	lettuce

2

The pizza has got:

mustard	lettuce
cheese	olives
tomato sauce	ice cream
chicken	mushrooms

3

The salad has got:

tomato sauce	cucumbers
turkey	milk
lettuce	cheese
onions	chicken
green peppers	tomatoes

30 **Look at 29 and answer.**

1 Is there any lettuce in the sandwich? _____

2 Is there any mustard on the pizza? _____

3 Are there any olives on the pizza? _____

4 Are there any onions in the salad? _____

31 **Write about your home.**

1 Are there any tomatoes in your fridge? _____

2 Is there any milk in your fridge? _____

Healthy Living

 1 Write. Use activities from the box. Then ✓ the healthy ones.

ate a healthy breakfast	ate pie for breakfast	drank lots of water
got ten hours of sleep	got two hours of sleep	rode a bike

1 _____
_____ ☐

2 _____
_____ ☐

3 _____
_____ ☐

4 _____
_____ ☐

5 _____
_____ ☐

6 _____
_____ ☐

2 Read and circle for you.

1 How do you feel today? I feel **great / awful / OK** today.

2 Did you get enough sleep? **Yes / No**

3 Did you eat any breakfast? **Yes / No**

4 Did you drink lots of water? **Yes / No**

5 Did you ride your bike? **Yes / No**

6 Did you have a healthy lunch? **Yes / No**

7 Did you do any exercise? **Yes / No**

3 **Listen and write.**

| any | Did | enough | good | too | you |

Live Right!

Did you eat breakfast? asks Mum,
You don't look ¹_____ to me.
Did you get ²_____ sleep? asks Mum,
Did you watch ³_____much TV?

Enough sleep. Good food.
Be healthy. Live right!
Enough sleep. Good food.
Be healthy. Live right!

⁴_____ you ride your bike? asks Mum,
You know it's good for ⁵_____.
Did you get ⁶_____ exercise?
You know it's good to do!

Chorus

4 **Read and ✓ for you. Then answer with Yes, I did or No, I didn't.**

My Habits Last Week	Sun	Mon	Tue	Wed	Thu	Fri	Sat
1 got enough sleep							
2 drank enough water							
3 ate healthy food							

Did you get enough sleep? _____

Did you drink enough water? _____

Did you eat enough healthy food? _____

5 **Read and answer. Write Yes, she did or No, she didn't.**

An Unhealthy Dinner

Amy's dad wants her to be healthy. Amy likes unhealthy food. She ate burger and chips for her dinner. Fried food isn't healthy. She drank a large cola. Cola isn't healthy. It's got lots of sugar. Now, Amy doesn't feel very well.

1 Did Amy eat burger and chips for dinner? _____

2 Did she eat fried food? _____

3 Did she drink a large glass of water? _____

4 Did she eat a healthy dinner? _____

6 **What did you eat for dinner yesterday? Was it healthy? Draw, write and circle.**

Yesterday for dinner, I ate _____

and I drank _____.

My dinner **was / wasn't** healthy.

THINK BIG **Healthy or unhealthy? Draw.**

chips   lettuce   tomatoes   bottle of cola   burger   water

156
7 **Listen and stick. What did Grace and Carlos do at the weekend?**

Sunday

1 _____

Saturday

Sunday

2 _____   **3** _____

8 **Read and complete with did or didn't.**

1 **Lou:** Are you feeling OK?

Jack: I'm tired.

Lou: _____ you exercise today?

Jack: No, I _____. I played video
games all day.

Lou: Oh. _____ you sleep eight hours?

Jack: No, I _____. I slept four hours.

2 **Ellen:** Hi, Jim. I feel great today! How are you?

Jim: Not good. I _____ eat a good breakfast.

Ellen: What _____ you eat?

Jim: I ate ice cream and I drank cola.

Ellen: Really? What _____ you eat for lunch?

Jim: I forgot lunch. I _____ eat lunch.

9 **Look and circle.**

| Yesterday Morning | Yesterday Afternoon | Yesterday Evening |

1 They **ate dinner** / **woke up** yesterday evening.

2 They **watched TV** / **woke up** yesterday afternoon.

3 They **ate dinner** / **woke up** yesterday morning.

10 **Look and answer.**

1 Did he get enough sleep? _____

2 Did she get enough sleep? _____

3 Did they get enough exercise? _____

4 Did she eat a healthy dinner? _____

5 Did he eat a healthy dinner? _____

6 Did she drink any water? _____

7 Did he drink enough water? _____

11 **Read and complete. Use the words from the box.**

| active | activities | energy | measure | put on weight | watching TV |

A calorie is a ¹_____ of the energy we get from food. We need calories to give us ²_____ to do different activities and sports. Some ³_____ , such as riding a bike and dancing, use a lot of calories and are really good for us. Sleeping and ⁴_____ don't use any calories. If we eat more calories than we use, we can ⁵_____ so it's important to stay ⁶_____ .

158

12 **Read and circle. Then listen and check.**

1   It's important to eat, exercise, rest and sleep every day. Food and drink give us energy because they have ¹ **muscles / calories** in them. A calorie is a ² **measure / activity** of this energy.

2   Some foods have a lot of calories and some don't. We need to have a certain number of calories to be ³ **fat / healthy**. If we have too many calories and don't use the energy, we can ⁴ **take / put on** weight and become ⁵ **tired / fat**. Exercise uses the energy by burning calories.

3   Being active and doing exercise at any age is also good for the heart, our ⁶ **bones / feet** and our ⁷ **teeth / muscles**. Activities like swimming, cycling, dancing, running and walking are good for burning calories and keeping us fit. Sitting down at the computer too much or watching too much TV isn't good for your body.

4   Sleeping is important to give your body and brain time to ⁸ **play / rest**. The next day we can continue to be active and work or study. Too much or too little sleep can be bad for your ⁹ **exercise / health**. Doctors say between 9 and 10 hours of sleep is best for teenagers.

5   We must always try to find time to ¹⁰ **watch television / exercise** and to rest. We must always watch what we eat. It's OK to have sweets or chocolate from time to time but, as they have a lot of calories, they aren't healthy foods.

13 **Look at 12. Read and match.**

1 Calories are measures of energy

2 When we are active, our body

3 Cycling or walking is good for us

4 Too many calories

5 Sleep is important because

a can make us fat if we don't exercise.

b but watching too much TV is unhealthy.

c our body and brain can rest.

d and are in the things we eat and drink.

e burns calories to take the energy we need.

14 **Complete the diagram. Add five more activities.**

dancing   doing gymnastics   playing basketball   playing video games
playing tennis   riding a bike   running   sleeping   watching a DVD

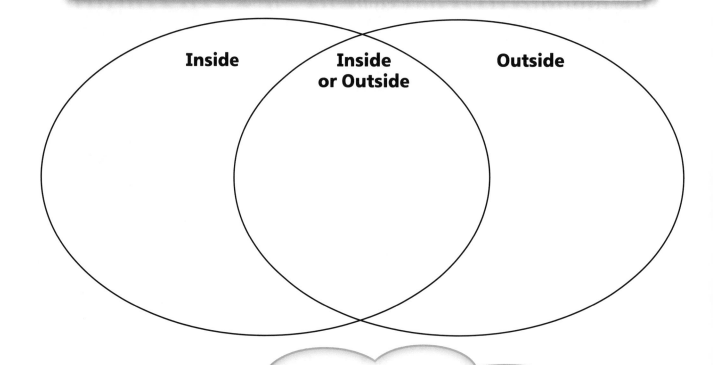

Inside

Inside or Outside

Outside

 THINK BIG   **Read and choose.**

1 Sleep for **eight** / **twelve** hours a day.

2 Play **six hours** / **one hour** of football a day.

3 Eat a **big** / **small** breakfast.

15 **Complete the chart. Use the words from the box.**

> arrive   clap   control   cook   dry   fry   jog
> live   look   love   study   work

climbed	tried	changed	dropped

16 **Read and write.**

1 eat _____ate_____

2 get _____

3 hurt _____

4 make _____

5 ride _____

6 run _____

7 say _____

8 sit _____

9 swim _____

10 wake _____

17 **Read and write. Use the correct form of the verb in brackets.**

When Josh ¹ _____ (come) home, he ² _____ (go) to bed and ³ _____ (sleep) for ten hours. He ⁴ _____ (be) so tired. When he ⁵ _____ (get) up, he ⁶ _____ (eat) a big breakfast and then ⁷ _____ (ride) his bike for an hour. He ⁸ _____ (visit) his favourite café and ⁹ _____ (drink) some apple juice. He ¹⁰ _____ (see) some friends in the afternoon. In the evening, he ¹¹ _____ (tidy) his room and then ¹² _____ (start) to watch a film. But he ¹³ _____ (fall) asleep in the first ten minutes!

18 Complete the questions and answers.

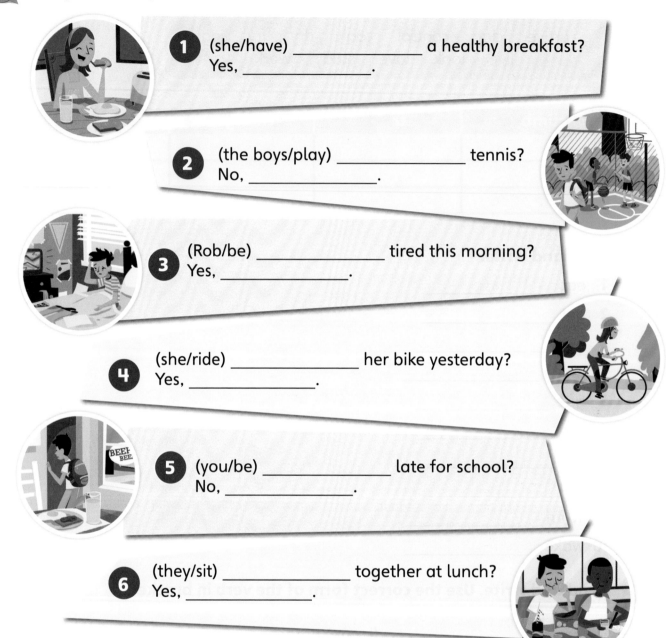

1 (she/have) _____ a healthy breakfast?
Yes, _____ .

2 (the boys/play) _____ tennis?
No, _____ .

3 (Rob/be) _____ tired this morning?
Yes, _____ .

4 (she/ride) _____ her bike yesterday?
Yes, _____ .

5 (you/be) _____ late for school?
No, _____ .

6 (they/sit) _____ together at lunch?
Yes, _____ .

19 Write negative sentences.

1 He drank lots of water.

_____

2 We forgot to invite the neighbours.

_____

3 They got a letter from the bank.

_____

20 **Read and match.**

Octopush

Pumpkin Regatta

Footvolley

1 Octopush is like hockey

2 A pumpkin regatta is like a boat race

3 Footvolley is like volleyball

a but people don't race in boats.

b but the players use a football.

c but people play it underwater.

161

21 **Listen, read and write.**

| kick   net   regattas   rowing   score   Teams |

1   Octopush is like hockey but people play it underwater in a swimming pool. A scuba diving club invented it in 1954 when it was too cold to go in the sea. The game started in England, but now people play it all over the world. You need eight players to play. **1** _____ use sticks to push a puck or 'squid' into a net to **2** _____ points.

2   Footvolley is just like volleyball but players use a football. The game started in Brazil on Copacabana Beach in 1965. Police always stopped people playing football on the beach, so people played on volleyball courts instead. They invented footvolley. You have to **3** _____ the ball over the **4** _____ and you can't touch it with your hands. It's exciting but difficult. Many famous Brazilian footballers also play footvolley.

3   In the autumn, in parts of the United States and Canada, there's a contest called a Pumpkin Regatta. It's a boat race but people use giant, hollowed out pumpkins instead! It started in 1999 in Windsor in Nova Scotia. A man there grew giant pumpkins and he decided to use them for **5** _____. Pumpkin racing became very popular, and soon other places raced their own **6** _____. The pumpkins weigh more than 450 kilograms. After the race, there's usually a pumpkin pie-eating contest.

22 **Read and match.**

1 Scuba divers in England started octopush

2 In octopush, the players use sticks

3 Footvolley started when the police stopped

4 A man grew giant pumpkins

5 When the races finish,

a people playing football on the beach.

b and hollowed them out to use them as boats.

c because the sea was too cold.

d people eat pumpkin pies.

e to push a puck into the net to score.

23 **Read and circle T for true and F for false.**

1 Octopush is a game where you need eight points to win.   T   F

2 In footvolley, you can use your hands and your feet.   T   F

3 The police said that people couldn't play football on the beach.   T   F

4 In a pumpkin regatta, people row their boats to race against pumpkins.   T   F

5 After regattas, people eat pumpkin pie.   T   F

THINK BIG

Make up a strange sport. Draw and describe it.

The sport is called

_____

_____.

24 **Read and circle.**

1 I usually walk to school **or / but** today I rode my bike.

2 I sometimes play tennis **and / but** baseball after school.

3 I can walk to school **or / but** I can take a bus to school.

4 I like dancing **and / but** I'm not very good at it.

5 I usually get eight **and / or** nine hours of sleep.

6 It's hot **but / and** sunny today.

25 **Read and write. Use the ideas from the box.**

> and I help her do the dishes
> but he isn't good at basketball
> but she sounds terrible
> or I take the bus

1 My friend always plays the guitar _____.

2 My brother is good at flying kites _____.

3 My dad drives me to school _____.

4 I help my mum cook dinner _____.

26 **Read and complete with or, but or and.**

I think I live a healthy life. I love doing exercise ¹_____ playing sports. I usually play tennis ²_____ volleyball on Saturday ³_____ when it's rainy I go running inside in a gym. I sometimes have a burger ⁴_____ chips for lunch ⁵_____ I usually eat turkey and rice ⁶_____ pizza and salad.

27 **Read and circle all, au and aw.**

ball

haul

cry

yawn

draw

tall

prince

claw

28 **Underline the words with all, au and aw. Then read aloud.**

1 Paul, don't kick the ball to the wall.

2 Draw a tiger with big claws.

29 **Connect the letters. Then write.**

1 sm   aul   **a** _ _ _ _

2 dr   all   **b** _ _ _ _ _

3 h   aw   **c** _ _ _ _

167
30 **Listen and write.**

I'm **¹** _____, I'm bored.

Yawn, **²** _____.

Let's play, let's play

With a **³** _____,

Let's **⁴** _____,

Let's draw a **⁵** _____.

31 **Circle the correct verb.**

1 Did they **eat / ate** a healthy lunch?

2 She **drink / drank** enough water today.

3 She didn't **play / played** volleyball today.

32 **Read and complete. Use the words from the box.**

| any | didn't | enough | got | healthy | rode |

1 John didn't get _____ sleep last night. He woke up at 4 a.m.
2 John _____ eat breakfast this morning.
3 John didn't get _____ exercise today. He watched TV all day.
4 Sue _____ enough sleep last night.
5 Sue ate a _____ breakfast this morning.
6 Sue _____ her bike to school today.

33 **Complete the sentences. Use the words in brackets.**

1 _____ football is good fun and it's good for my health. (play)
2 _____ is good for your body. (run)
3 _____ my bike is good for my health. (ride)
4 _____ is important. But don't sleep too much! (sleep)
5 _____ turkey and rice is good for me. (eat)

unit 9 School Trips!

1 **Look and write.**

| aquarium | art gallery | dairy farm | museum | national park | zoo |

1 _____

2 _____

3 _____

4 _____

5 _____

6 _____

2 **Look, read and circle. Then number.**

1 We went to a national park. We learned about
   a penguins.   **b** rocks.   **c** music.

2 We went to the zoo. We saw
   a dinosaurs.   **b** elephants.   **c** paintings.

3 We went to a dairy farm. We learned about
   a rocks.   **b** paintings.   **c** cows.

4 We went to a concert hall. We heard
   a some music.   **b** sea lions.   **c** some cows.

3 **Listen and number in order.**

Learning Out of School

Where did you go?
What did you see?
We went to the zoo, we saw a play,
We had a great time!

I like going on school trips,
Learning out of school.
We go to lots of places.
They're interesting and cool!

**School trips. School trips.
They're a lot of fun.
School trips. School trips.
Let's go on one!**

Aquarium, theatre, concert hall and zoo,
We saw some great things.
There was lots to do!

Chorus

4 **Write.**

My favourite school trip is _____.

5 **Read and write.**

| art gallery concert hall dairy farm theatre zoo |

1 I didn't see any giraffes but I saw a hippo and zebra.

_____

2 I learned about French artists. _____

3 I saw a play about animals. _____

4 We saw about five hundred cows! They were

smelly. _____

5 There were drums, violins and guitars there and the

music was great. _____

6 **Read. Then write Luke or Amy.**

A Cool Trip

Luke and Amy went on a trip. They went to the Red Rock National Park. They learned about many kinds of rocks. Amy liked the trip a lot. Luke didn't like the trip. He didn't like the rocks and he didn't like walking. Amy got a present for Luke. It was a rock!

1 _____ really liked the trip.

2 _____ didn't like the trip.

3 _____ didn't like the rocks.

4 _____ got a present for her brother.

7 **Imagine a school trip. Then answer.**

1 Where did you go?

_____

2 When did you go?

_____

3 What did you see?

_____

4 Did you like the trip?

_____

What happens next in the story? Write.

THINK BIG

_____

_____

_____

8 **176** **Listen and stick.**

a

b

c

d

9 **Write. Complete the dialogue.**

A: Where ¹_____ you go on
your school trip?

B: We ²_____ to a dairy farm.

A: What ³_____ you see?

B: We saw farmers milk cows.

A: Did you ⁴_____ it?

B: No, I ⁵_____.
The cows smelled awful!

10 **Think about a trip you took. Draw and answer.**

Where did you go?

You: _____

What did you see?

You: _____

What did you do?

You: _____

11 **Complete. Then match.**

heard   learned   saw (x2)

1 _____ a film about dinosaurs   **a** national park

2 _____ a play about animals   **b** concert hall

3 _____ about rocks and nature   **c** museum

4 _____ some music   **d** theatre

12 **Read and match. Make questions.**

1 What   **a** did they go?

2 Did   **b** did they see?

3 Where   **c** they like it?

13 **Look at 12. Write the questions. Imagine the answers.**

1 A: _____

B: _____

2 A: _____

B: _____

3 A: _____

B: _____

14 **Look at the paintings. Match.**

a   b   c   d

1 *Old Man with his Head in his Hands*, by Vincent Van Gogh.

2 *Haystacks at Giverny*, by Claude Monet.

3 *Spring 1573*, by Giuseppe Arcimboldo.

4 *The Little Giants*, by Francisco de Goya.

178

15 **Listen, read and write.**

> century   copy   Dutch   impressionist
> Museum   nature   painting   watercolour

1   On her visit to the National Gallery, Amy's favourite ¹ _____ was *Spring 1573* by Giuseppe Arcimboldo. Arcimboldo was an Italian artist and he painted *Spring 1573* in the 16th century. He painted a face that has fruit, vegetables and flowers. It's very clever because it shows the connection between people and ² _____. Amy thought it was pretty and colourful.

2   Nina loves a painting called *The Little Giants* from the Prada ³ _____ in Madrid. It's by the Spanish artist Francisco de Goya. It's from the 19th ⁴ _____ and shows some children playing a game. The young children are happy but the older children look sad. The artist lost his hearing soon after he finished this painting.

3   Asya likes the painting *Haystacks at Giverny* by Claude Monet. He was a French ⁵ _____ painter. The original is in the Musée d'Orsay in Paris. Asya's grandmother has a ⁶ _____ of it in her living room. The picture shows a farm, she thinks, and makes her think of summer.

4   Monique likes *Old Man with his Head in his Hands* by Vincent Van Gogh. Van Gogh was ⁷ _____ and the painting is in a museum near where she lived. It's a sketch with ⁸ _____ from 1882. She finds it sad to look at but also interesting. She thinks something bad happened so it scares her a little. Van Gogh was very ill when he painted it.

16 **Look at 15. Circle T for true and F for false.**

1 *Spring 1573* is a picture of a person's face with food and flowers.　**T**　**F**

2 All the children in *The Little Giants* are happy.　**T**　**F**

3 The artist Francisco de Goya went deaf.　**T**　**F**

4 Asya's grandmother has a copy of *Haystacks at Giverny*
   in her house.　**T**　**F**

5 *Old Man with his Head in his Hands* is an oil painting.　**T**　**F**

6 Monique doesn't feel happy when she looks at the painting by
   Van Gogh.　**T**　**F**

17 **Read and match.**

1 Amy thinks the painting
   is clever because

2 In the painting, there
   are some children playing

3 The painting makes
   Asya think

4 Van Gogh's painting is
   a sketch in watercolour,

a it shows a connection between
      people and nature.

b of summer.

c so it wasn't made with oils.

d but some look happy and
      some look sad.

THINK BIG

Choose one of the painters. Find out information about
one more of his paintings and write.

The painting's name is _____ and it was

painted in _____ by _____.

In the painting, there is/are _____

and _____. I think the painting looks

_____.

18 **Read and write. Use the past tense of the verbs in brackets.**

The school trip ¹ _____ (be) great.
We ² _____ (visit) the zoo. We
³ _____ (see) lots of animals and
⁴ _____ (learn) a lot. Some monkeys
⁵ _____ (jump) on our bus! They
⁶ _____ (like) playing with us. We
⁷ _____ (try) to get them off but
they ⁸ _____ (stay) on the bus all
the time! Then we ⁹ _____ (stop)
at the café to rest. We ¹⁰ _____
(drink) some water and ¹¹ _____
(have) a little snack to eat. We
¹² _____ (be) so hungry! After
our break, we ¹³ _____ (go) round the reptile house. I liked
the big snakes. I ¹⁴ _____ (get) a DVD from the souvenir shop.

19 **Look at 18. Make negative sentences.**

1 The school trip _____ great.

2 We _____ the zoo.

3 Some monkeys _____ on our bus.

4 They _____ playing with us.

5 We _____ to get them off.

6 They _____ on the bus all the time.

7 We _____ at the café.

8 We _____ water and we _____ a snack.

9 I _____ the big snakes.

10 I _____ a DVD from the souvenir shop.

20 **Make questions and write answers.**

1 you visit/aquarium/on Saturday

A: _Did you visit the aquarium on Saturday?_____?

  ✗ aquarium   ✓ zoo

B: _I didn't visit the aquarium but I visited the zoo._____._

2 he go/theatre/last night

A: _____?

  ✗ theatre   ✓ cinema

B: _____.

3 they play/computer games/last weekend

A: _____?

  ✗ computer games ✓ chess

B: _____.

4 she see/*The Lego Movie*/yesterday

A: _____?

  ✗ *The Lego Movie* ✓ *The Boxtrolls*

B: _____.

5 you buy/T-shirt/this morning

A: _____?

  ✗ T-shirt   ✓ jumper

B: _____.

21 **Write questions using Why.**

1 Her teacher wasn't at school today.

_Why wasn't her teacher at school today?_____

2 You didn't get the bus.

_____

3 She didn't call the police.

_____

4 He didn't get more eggs.

_____

22 **Look and write.**

flamenco   Mua Roi Nuoc   Shakespeare play

1 _____   2 _____   3 _____

181

23 **Read and write. Then listen and check.**

actors   audiences   Cinema   magical   plays   shows   stage   theatre

1   People love entertainment. ¹ _____ and TV are new kinds of entertainment but entertainment on ² _____ is much older. Theatres are still very popular all over the world.

2   The Greeks had theatres more than 2,000 years ago, in almost every city. The ³ _____ had important things to say about life. They were sometimes funny or sad and only had men or boys as ⁴ _____. They usually had a chorus with people singing. Greek plays are still popular today.

3   Going to the ⁵ _____ became very popular about 400 years ago because of William Shakespeare. He wrote many different and clever plays, which people still watch and love today. People laugh or feel sad about the same things as the ⁶ _____ of his time. One of his most famous plays is *Romeo and Juliet*.

4   Stage ⁷ _____ with music and dance are also very popular. In Spain, people enjoy flamenco music and dance. There's usually a guitar player and one or more singers. Then there are the palmeros, who sing and clap in a special way, while men and women dance. There's a story and the dancing and music are very dramatic.

5   Mua Roi Nuoc is theatre entertainment in Vietnam. The performances use only puppets on a stage filled with water. These shows began in the 11ᵗʰ century and people still watch them today. They're ⁸ _____.

24 **Read and match.**

1 Cinema and TV are popular

2 Greek plays were funny or sad

3 William Shakespeare wrote many plays

4 Flamenco dancing in Spain

5 Mua Roi Nuoc in Vietnam

a usually goes with guitar music and clapping.

b but they are not as old as theatre entertainment.

c is very old and only uses puppets.

d and made going to the theatre popular.

e and usually had a chorus with singing.

25 **Find the words. Use them to complete the sentences.**

atesg   earteth   ncdae   upeptsp   ylsap

1 Flamenco is a Spanish _____.

2 Mua Roi Nuoc is a Vietnamese show with _____.

3 _____ became popular in England 400 years ago.

4 William Shakespeare's _____ are still very popular today.

5 The music for flamenco is usually played on a _____.

What stories do you like in cinema or theatre? Happy, sad, romantic, action or adventure? Write three sentences about why you like them.

THINK
BIG   _____

_____

_____

26 **Underline subjects in red, verbs in blue and objects in purple.**

1 Sally and Craig went to the zoo.

2 I didn't see a sea lion show.

3 My parents went out for dinner.

4 We visited an art gallery.

5 Did you see any rocks?

27 **What's missing? Write S for subject, V for verb and O for object. Then look and complete.**

> I   learned   like   paintings   they

1 They saw lots of _____. ☐

2 We didn't _____ the play. ☐

3 _____ watched a film today. ☐

4 Ali and Peter _____ about dinosaurs. ☐

5 Did _____ like it? ☐

28 **Put the paragraph in order. Now write your own.**

I want to go again. It was great fun!

A Trip to the Aquarium ☐

First, we saw penguins and turtles. Then we saw lots of sharks. These were my favourite. There was a whale show and it was amazing. I took some photos and we loved it.

In my school, we go on school trips every month. ☐

☐

☐

_____

_____

_____

_____

_____

Phonics | nt, ld, nd, st

29 **Read and circle nt, ld, nd and st.**

plant

ant

child

call

hand

nest

cold

draw

fast

band

30 **Underline the words with nt, ld, nd and st. Then read aloud.**

1 Put your hands in your pockets. It's cold.

2 This is an ant's nest.

31 **Connect the letters. Then write.**

1 pla   ld   **a** _ _ _ _

2 co   nd   **b** _ _ _ _

3 ha   st   **c** _ _ _ _

4 ne   nt   **d** _ _ _ _ _

187
32 **Listen and write.**

An ¹ _____ ,

² _____

³ _____ playing

In the ⁴ _____ .

A ⁵ _____

⁶ _____ playing in

A ⁷ _____ .

33 **Read the clues and write the places.**

1 The paintings were beautiful here.

_____

2 I learned about penguins and zebras.

_____

3 The music sounds amazing.

_____

4 We saw sea lions and sharks.

_____

34 **Find the five adjectives. Use them to make sentences.**

avuwfunnysfionboringjomsinterestingxicqscaryeapostrangetyur

1 I think _____ **is / are** _____ because _____

_____ .

2 I think _____ .

3 I _____ .

4 _____ .

5 _____ .

35 **Complete the dialogues.**

1 **A:** My parents ¹_____ to a play last night. (go)

B: ²_____ they like it? (do)

A: Yes, they ³_____! (do)

B: ⁴_____ you in the play? (be)

A: Yes, I ⁵_____! (be)

2 **A:** Where ¹_____ you yesterday? (be)

B: We ²_____ to the museum. (go)

A: Did you ³_____ fun? (have)

B: No, we ⁴_____. (do not) We ⁵_____ it. (not like)

Matt's Day

1 **Look at the paths for Matt's day and complete the faces.**

 = healthy   😟 = unhealthy

2 **Choose one path. Draw the path. Learn about Matt's day.**

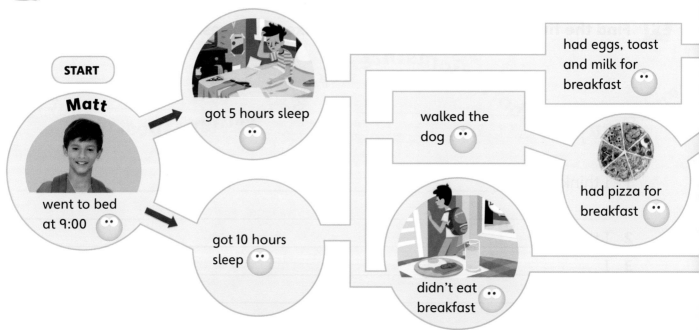

START

Matt

went to bed at 9:00

got 5 hours sleep

got 10 hours sleep

walked the dog

didn't eat breakfast

had eggs, toast and milk for breakfast

had pizza for breakfast

3 **Look at your path in 2. What do you think? Write the answers.**

1 What time did Matt wake up? _____

2 Did Matt get enough sleep? _____

3 Did Matt get enough exercise? _____

4 Did Matt eat healthy food? _____

5 Where did Matt go on the school trip? What did he do? _____

_____

6 How did Matt feel in the evening? _____

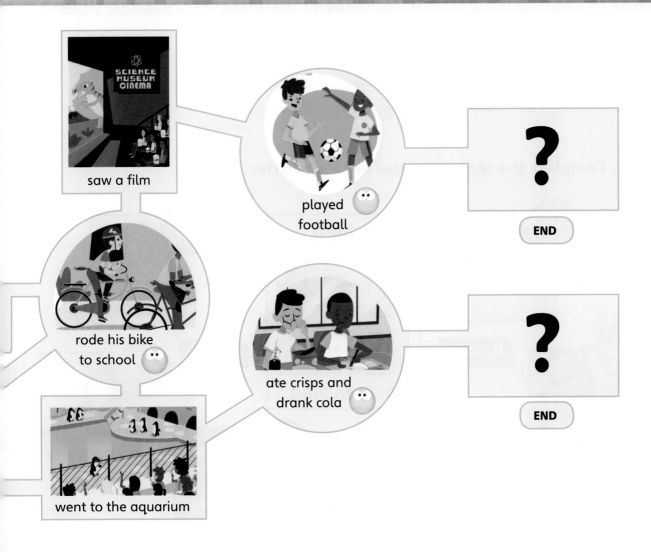

saw a film

played football

rode his bike to school

ate crisps and drank cola

went to the aquarium

?

END

?

END

4 Use your path in 2. Write a paragraph about Matt's day. Write a title.

_____

_____

_____

_____

_____

_____

_____

_____

What does he/she do **before** school?	He/She eats breakfast **before** school.
What do you do **after** school?	I play football **after** school.

1 **Look. Complete the sentences. Use before or after.**

School

Before

After

8:30 to 3:00

1 She plays video games _____ school.

2 What does she do _____ school? She wakes up.

3 She always gets dressed _____ school.

4 What does he have _____ school? He has cereal.

5 He always watches TV _____ school.

6 What does she do _____ school? She does her homework.

2 **Write about your family.**

1 What does your mother do in the morning? _____

2 What does your father do in the evening? _____

What does he/she **do**?	He/She **is** a nurse.
Where does he/she **work**?	He/She **works** at a hospital.
What do your sisters **do**?	They'**re** (They **are**) nurses.

1 **Look. Circle and complete the dialogues.**

| Pete | Uncle – waiter | Dad – firefighter | Mum – cashier | | Katrina | cousin – student | cousin – student |

1 **Katrina:** What **do / does** your father do?

Pete: He's a _____.

Katrina: Where **do / does** he work?

Pete: He **work / works** at a fire station.

2 **Pete:** What **do / does** your cousins do?

Katrina: They're _____.

Pete: Where **do / does** they study?

Katrina: They **study / studies** at a university.

3 **Katrina:** _____

Pete: He's a waiter.

Katrina: _____

Pete: He _____ at a restaurant.

4 **Katrina:** _____

Pete: She's a cashier.

Katrina: _____

Pete: She works at a supermarket.

| What **does** he/she **have to** do? | He/She **has to** feed the fish. |
| What **do** you/we/they **have to** do? | I/We/You/They **have to** feed the fish. |

1 **Look. Complete the questions and answers.**

All tasks
May 14th
Matt to do: feed the cat twice today
Lucy and David to do: clean their rooms
Lucy and I to do: do the dishes
Lucy to do: practise the piano after school

1 **A:** What does Matt have to do?

   B: He _____.

2 **A:** What do Lucy and David have to do?

   B: They _____.

3 **A:** What _____ Lucy and I _____?

   B: You _____.

4 **A:** What _____ Lucy _____?

   B: She _____.

| I/You/We/They | **always** **usually** | do the dishes. |
| He/She | **sometimes** **never** | takes out the rubbish. |

2 **Look. Write never, usually or always.**

Everyday Habits	Mon	Tues	Wed	Thurs	Fri
1 We _____ eat a good breakfast.	✓	✓	✓	✓	✓
2 She _____ plays tennis after school.					
3 I _____ wake up late.	✓	✓	✓	✓	

What **can** a penguin do?	It **can** swim. It **can't** fly.	subject + *can/can't* + verb
What **can** bears do?	They **can** climb. They **can't** fly.	
Can a penguin swim?	Yes, it **can**.	subject + *can/can't*
Can bears fly?	No, they **can't**.	

1 **Write one animal name in each box in the chart.**

a bear   a camel   a snake   lizards   penguins   sea lions

What Can They Do?	Can	Can't
1 live in ice and snow		
2 do tricks		
3 live in deserts		

2 **Look at 1. Complete the dialogues.**

1 **A:** _____ a penguin _____ in ice and snow?

  B: Yes, _____ but a camel _____.

3 **A:** What _____ a camel _____?

  B: _____ live in deserts.

5 **A:** _____ a bear live in forests?

  B: _____.

2 **A:** What can lizards do?

  B: They _____ live in deserts.

4 **A:** Can a bear live in deserts?

  B: No, it _____.

6 **A:** What _____ sea lions _____?

  B: Sea lions _____ tricks but they _____ talk.

| What **is** the weather like today? | It**'s** hot and sunny. |
| What **was** the weather **like** yesterday? | It **was** sunny. We **were** warm. |

 Look. Complete the questions and answers.

Carla

Barcelona, Spain	
Yesterday	Today
32°C	32°C

Massi

Algiers, Algeria	
Yesterday	Today
23°C	20°C

Yoko

Sapporo, Japan	
Yesterday	Today
10°C	5°C

1 Massi: What _____ the weather like today in Barcelona?

Carla: It _____ hot and rainy.

2 Yoko: What _____ the weather like yesterday in Algiers?

Massi: It _____ warm and cloudy.

3 Carla: _____ today in Sapporo?

Yoko: _____

2 Look at 1. Complete the dialogues.

1 A: _____

B: It was hot and sunny.

2 A: What's the weather like today in Algiers?

B: _____

3 A: What was the weather like in Sapporo yesterday?

B: _____

How **does** the apple pie **taste**?	It **tastes** delicious.
How **do** your new shoes **feel**?	They **feel** good.

1 **Look. Match the words and write the sentences.**

1   2   3   4

1 The flowers   looks   awful. _____

2 The cheese   smell   tight. _____

3 The shoes   look   nice. _____

4 The shirt   smells   comfortable. _____

2 **Write the questions.**

1 **A:** _____

B: The music sounds nice.

2 **A:** _____

B: The biscuits taste delicious.

3 **A:** _____

B: The scarf feels soft.

4 **A:** _____

B: The perfume smells nice.

Is there **any** pizza?	Yes, there is **some** pizza.	Are there **any** onions?	Yes, there are **some** onions.
Is there **any** fish?	No, there isn't **any** fish.	Are there **any** eggs?	No, there aren't **any** eggs.

1 **Look and write.**

Special Today!

_____

_____

_____

_____

bread
cucumber
lettuce
mustard

2 **Look at 1. Write some or any.**

1 There is _____ lettuce.

2 There isn't _____ tomato sauce.

3 There aren't _____ tomatoes.

4 There are _____ cucumbers.

3 **Write questions and answers. Then draw the sandwich.**

1 Are there _____ bananas?

Yes, there are _____ bananas.

2 _____ onions?

No, there aren't _____ onions.

3 _____ yoghurt?

_____ yoghurt.

4 _____ chips?

_____ chips.

Silly Sandwich

Did you/he/she/they **get** enough sleep yesterday?	Yes, I/he/she/they **did**.	No, I/he/she/they **didn't**

1 **Read and match.**

1	Did you have	**a**	to the zoo?
2	Did they eat	**b**	Sue ride their bikes?
3	Did she go	**c**	you see any rocks?
4	Did he	**d**	a healthy lunch?
5	Did	**e**	visit a museum?
6	Did Al and	**f**	fun?

2 **Look. Write questions and answers.**

1 **A:** Did Matt eat any breakfast?

   B: No, _____ .

2 **A:** _____ enough sleep?

   B: No, _____ .

3 **A:** Did Sue have a big breakfast?

   B: Yes, _____ .

4 **A:** _____ some exercise?

   B: Yes, _____ .

Where **did** you/he/she/they **go**?	I/He/She/They **went** to the Science Museum.	
What **did** you/he/she/they **see**?	I/He/She/They **saw** an interesting film about dinosaurs.	
Did you/he/she/they **like** it?	Yes, I/he/she/they **liked** it.	No, I/he/she/they **didn't like** it.

1 **Find and circle the past form of the verbs. Then match.**

l   g   r   d   r   a   n   k   z   **1** eat

a   t   e   m   z   m   l   k   o   **2** do

p   o   n   h   a   d   x   u   i   **3** drink

i   n   e   h   r   g   d   i   d   **4** get

a   f   g   c   g   o   t   s   w   **5** have

z   x   c   v   b   r   o   d   e   **6** ride

2 **Look and circle. Then answer.**

Jeff and Jack

Tim

1 Where did Jeff and Jack **go / went** yesterday? _____

2 What did they **see / saw**? _____

3 Where **does / did** Tim go last weekend? _____

4 **Does / Did** Tim like it? _____

Young Learners English Practice Movers: Listening A

– 5 questions –

Listen and draw lines. There is one example.

Mary   John   Vicky   Fred

Jack   Sally

Young Learners English Practice Movers: Listening B

– 5 questions –

 Listen and tick (✔) the box. There is one example.

What is his job?

A ☐   B ✔   C ☐

1 What is her job?

A ☐   B ☐   C ☐

2 What time does she usually stop working?

A ☐   B ☐   C ☐

3 What does she have to do every day?

A ☐

B ☐

C ☐

4 What does she like about her job?

A ☐

B ☐

C ☐

5 What job would she like to have in the future?

A ☐

B ☐

C ☐

Young Learners English Practice Movers: Listening C

 Listen and write. There is one example.

Susie's School Trip

What Susie did today: _____ *went on a school trip* _____

1 Where she went: _____

2 What she did in the morning: _____

3 What she had for lunch: _____

4 What she did in the afternoon: _____

5 What she learned: _____

Young Learners English Practice Movers: Reading & Writing A

Read the text. Choose the correct words and write them on the lines.

Example   Bears live in many different kinds of places around the ___world___. Some bears live in forests and mountains. Grizzly bears, for example, live in the Rocky Mountains, in the United States.

1   They explore when the _____ is warm and they sleep during the long

2   winter. They _____ climb trees and catch fish.

Polar bears live in the Arctic, where it's

3   _____ and cold all year round.

4   They've got thick _____ to protect them from the cold and they

5   hunt for fish under the _____. Like all other bears, they fit right into their environment.

Example   ocean   desert   world

1   weather   water   world

2   can   should   will

3   snowy   hot   rainy

4   feathers   beaks   fur

5   rock   ice   wood

Young Learners English Practice Movers: Reading & Writing B

– 6 questions –

Read the story. Choose a word from the box. Write the correct word next to numbers 1–6. There is one example.

Today starts off like any other day for Paul. He _____*wakes up*_____ and

gets out of bed. Then he goes into the bathroom and

1_____. After that, he 2_____

and takes the bus to school. But something is different today. At lunch, he

doesn't have to wait in line. The other kids let him go to the front. After

school, Paul comes home. He usually has to 3_____ and

take him for a walk but today his sister does it for him. In the evening, Paul's

mum cooks his favourite dinner. He always has to 4_____

after dinner but today he gets a break. Instead of doing chores, he gets to

5_____ with his brother and sister. What's different about

today? It's Paul's birthday. He almost always 6_____ at

8 o'clock but today his parents let him stay up late and eat ice cream.

"I wish every day was like today," says Paul.

Example

wakes up

eats breakfast

play football

do the dishes

does homework

goes to bed

washes his face

feed the dog

play games

(7) Now choose the best name for the story.

Tick (✔) one box.

My Everyday Life ☐

A Very Special Day ☐

Time for a Break ☐

Young Learners English Practice Movers: Reading & Writing C

– 6 questions –

Look and read. Write *yes* or *no*.

Examples

It's cold and windy today.   *no*

People are watching a play.   *yes*

Questions

1 A woman is jogging.   _____

2 A family are having a picnic. _____

3 There are some sandwiches on a plate. _____

4 A girl is walking her dog.   _____

5 People are watching a film.   _____

6 There is some lemonade for sale. _____

Young Learners English Practice Movers: Speaking A

Wordlist

snack	76	tongue	96	brick	125	national park	144
yesterday	76	final sentence	102	cream	125	school trip	144
average	80	black	103	cry	125	theatre	144
climate	80	block	103	dream	125	zoo	144
extreme	80	blow	103	drive	125	had	145
opposite	80	flag	103	frog	125	interesting	145
temperature	80	flip-flops	103	grass	125	saw	145
tourist	80	fly	103	prince	125	went	145
sleep	81	glad	103	prize	125	learned	146
cricket	84	glass	103	troll	125	liked	146
sledge	84	glow	103			old	146
detail sentences	86	plant	103	**Unit 8**	**Page**	got	147
swim	86	play	103	healthy	128	walked	147
scar	87	plum	103	any	129	ate	149
scout	87			enough	129	beautiful	150
slim	87	**Unit 7**	**Page**	unhealthy	130	boring	150
slow	87	bread	112	bad	131	colourful	150
snail	87	cucumbers	112	active	134	French	150
swan	87	from	112	activities	134	funny	150
sweet	87	green	112	body	134	hand	150
		lettuce	112	calorie	134	scary	150
Unit 6	**Page**	mushrooms	112	measure	134	strange	150
awful	90	olives	112	put on weight	134	Flamenco	154
delicious	90	onions	112	ball	138	Vietnam	155
feel	90	peppers	112	call	138	object	156
flowers	90	tomato sauce	112	footvolley	138	ant	157
horrible	90	turkey	112	hockey	138	band	157
look	90	fridge	114	net	138	chest	157
lovely	90	surprise	115	octopush	138	child	157
nice	90	blood	118	pumpkin	138	cold	157
pie	90	bone	118	race	138	fast	157
smell	90	brain	118	throw	138	nest	157
soft	90	energy	118	claw	141	plant	157
sound	90	muscles	118	draw	141	sand	157
soup	90	skin	118	haul	141	tent	157
sweet	90	vitamin	118	tall	141		
taste	90	Australia	122	wall	141		
terrible	90	doughnut	122	yawn	141		
tight	90	fried eggs	122				
cold	93	Japan	122	**Unit 9**	**Page**		
danger	93	Mexico	122	aquarium	144		
avoid	96	Spain	122	art gallery	144		
brain	96	butter	124	concert hall	144		
echo	96	maple syrup	124	dairy farm	144		
information	96	pancake	124	museum	144		

ask a question with:

What time...

ask a question with:

ask a question with:

**in the morning /
afternoon / evening**

ask a question with:

**at ____:____
(time)**

ask a question with:

before work

ask a question with:

after work

answer with:

I...

answer with:

I always...

answer with:

I usually...

answer with:

answer with:

I never...

answer with:

I have to...

All About

_____
(animals)

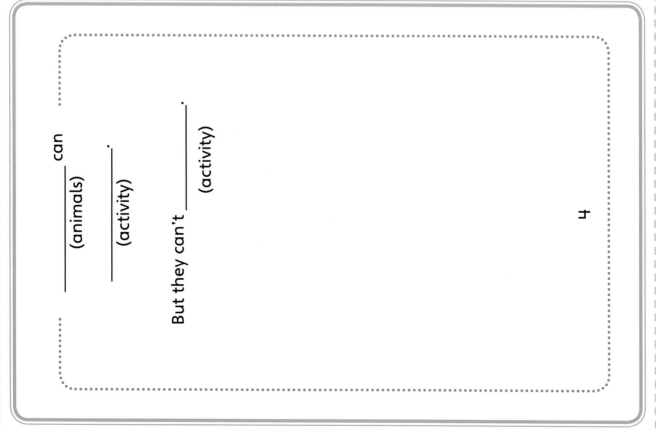

_____ can
(animals)

_____.
(activity)

But they can't _____.
(activity)

4

_____ live in
(animals)

_____ .
(habitat)

It's _____ there.
(weather word)

2

_____ eat
(animals)

_____ .
(food)

3

Dialogue 2

A: Did you eat breakfast this morning?

B: Yes, it was awesome. Sharks are cool!

A: Did you like it?

B: I ate turkey and lettuce.

A: What did you do there?

B: Yes, I had eggs on toast. I'm ready for the baseball game!

A: What did you eat for dinner?

B: We went to the aquarium.

A: Where did you go yesterday?

B: We saw a film about sharks.

3 My BIG ENGLISH World

My name: _____

My age: _____

My address: _____

My family: _____

ME

©2015 Pearson Education, Ltd.

ENGLISH
AROUND ME

Look around you. Paste or draw things with English words. Write everyday words.

Everyday Words
_____
_____
_____
_____
_____

FILM TICKET

Unit 1, page 5

Unit 2, page 19

Unit 3, page 33

Unit 4, page 49

Unit 5, page 63

Unit 6, page 77

Unit 7, page 93

Unit 8, page 107

Unit 9, page 121